DOUG STOWE

Rustic Furniture Basics

The Taunton Press

CALGARY PUBLIC LIBRARY

OCT — 2009   Nov 2012

D0472963

Text © 2009 by Doug Stowe

Photographs © 2009 by The Taunton Press, Inc.

Illustrations © 2009 by The Taunton Press, Inc.

All rights reserved.

The Taunton Press
Inspiration for hands-on living®

The Taunton Press, Inc., 63 South Main Street, PO Box 5506, Newtown, CT 06470-5506
e-mail: tp@taunton.com

Editor: Strother Purdy

Copy Editor: Seth Reichgott

Indexer: Cathy Goddard

Jacket/Cover design: Kimberly Adis

Interior design: Kimberly Adis

Layout: Cathy Cassidy

Illustrator: Robert LaPointe

Photographer: Doug Stowe

Library of Congress Cataloging-in-Publication Data

Stowe, Doug.
  Rustic furniture basics / Doug Stowe.
    p. cm.
  ISBN 978-1-60085-076-9
  1. Rustic woodwork. 2. Furniture making. 3. Country furniture. I. Title.
  TT200.S72 2009
  684.1'04--dc22

                    2009025350

Printed in the United States of America
10 9 8 7 6 5 4 3 2 1

The following manufacturers/names appearing in *Rustic Furniture Basics* are trademarks:
Bora Care®, Deft®, Duco®, Kreg®, Masonite®, Minwax®, Popsicle®, RotoZip®, Scotch-Brite®, Speed® Square,
Veritas®, Wood-Mizer®

Working with wood is inherently dangerous. Using hand or power tools improperly or ignoring safety practices can lead to permanent injury or even death. Don't try to perform operations you learn about here (or elsewhere) unless you're certain they are safe for you. If something about an operation doesn't feel right, don't do it. Look for another way. We want you to enjoy the craft, so please keep safety foremost in your mind whenever you're in the shop.

When I was just a kid, my father, mother, sisters, and I would go for walks along the Mississippi River at Memphis, Tennessee, picking up interesting pieces of driftwood. We used our imaginations, combining bits and pieces into new and interesting forms and found a great excuse to be outdoors on a Sunday afternoon.

I dedicate this book to those families like my own in which seeds are sown for personal creativity and love of nature and the outdoors.

ACKNOWLEDGMENTS

THE BEST BOOKS ARE ALWAYS A TEAM EFFORT, and I am honored to be part of a great team.

I offer my special thanks to my editor, Strother Purdy, and illustrator, Robert LaPointe. I also want to thank Helen Albert, Jessica DiDonato, and photo editor Katy Binder, all at Taunton Books. It has been a pleasure working with director Gary Junken on the DVD *Rustic Furniture Basics*. My thanks also to Wally Wilson and Rob Lee at Lee Valley/Veritas tools and Anne Thibeau at www.MilkPaint.com.

In addition, I want to thank other makers of rustic furniture for their example and inspiration. Just a few of these are: Daniel Mack, Paul Ruhlman, Greg Mitchell, Richard Bazeley, Barry Gregson, and Jack Hill.

Contents

INTRODUCTION

EACH PIECE OF WOOD TELLS THE STORY of the tree from which it came. Where there's a knot, there had been a branch. Where the grain is wide and straight, the tree had grown quickly, straight and tall. Where the grain is crooked or dense, the tree had grown in defiance of harsh circumstances.

We are storytellers, too, so it is not surprising we have a natural affinity with wood. When we make something from wood, we add the story of our understanding of the tools and our sensitivity to the materials. We also tell through our workmanship the story of the care we feel for others and ourselves.

The qualities of rustic work speak for themselves. Raw, rough qualities expressed as texture, random shape, and form offer a direct connection to the wondrous beauty of nature.

Whether you are a beginner making your first piece for a new home or an experienced craftsman exploring new creativity in the woodshop, you will find adventure in rustic work, and it is my hope that this book provides a foundation for your first step.

If you are a beginner, start at the beginning of this book. The projects are arranged in order of difficulty, and only a few common handyman tools are required for the early projects. Mix and match techniques between chapters and use the ideas presented in the variations to customize and personalize your own work. But don't forget to look beyond this book. Go out into the woods. You will find the forms and textures of the forest to be your greatest source of inspiration. Then don't be afraid to make mistakes. It is how we learn best.

Western Cedar Tables

WESTERN CEDAR is one of the few inexpensive roughsawn woods available from typical neighborhood lumberyards. When my wife and I bought our home, like most young couples we were on a tight budget and needed furniture. Western cedar came to the rescue.

These tables can be made so quickly that the joke in our house was that they could be made in five minutes. That, of course, wasn't true. But these tables, despite being quickly made, have been useful and beautiful for many years. The roughsawn wood, complete with knots and imperfections, never goes out of style. When I later made finer furniture to replace them, we passed them along to others starting out in their first homes.

Use the variations offered at the end of the chapter to inspire your own creativity beyond the basic design; with simple changes in the lengths and widths you can make tables for a variety of uses, both indoors and out.

Western cedar table

This table is sized for a bedside or end table and can be quickly made with common homeowner tools. Western cedar is one of the few roughsawn woods widely available from lumberyards. Pole barn spikes are used to secure the parts.

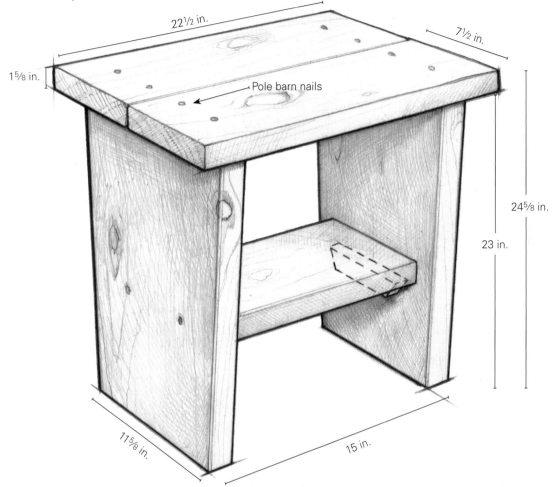

MATERIALS FOR END OR SIDE TABLE

QUANTITY	PART	SIZE	NOTES
2	Sides	1⅝ in. by 11⅝ in. by 23 in.	from 2×12 Western red cedar
1	Shelf	1⅝ in. by 7½ in. by 15 in.	
2	Shelf supports	¾ in. by 1½ in. by 6 in.	15-degree angle each end
2	Top	1⅝ in. by 7½ in. by 22½ in.	
12	Pole barn nails	6 in.	
8	#6 common nails		

Note: All materials from 2×8 Western red cedar unless noted.

Cut the stock to length

USE A SPEED SQUARE TO GUIDE the saw accurately as you square the ends. Hold the square tightly in place. The first cut is made close to the end of the stock. Turn the stock end for end, mark the length, and then align the guide and saw to cut at the mark.

ROUGH CUT PARTS LONGER than you need from stock. Use a carpenter's square and pencil or pen to mark a line and cut the stock by eye with a circular saw.

I USE A CIRCULAR SAW to cut the parts to length, but a handsaw will work nearly as well. Using sawhorses to hold the stock is an improvement over working on the ground, but don't let a lack of sawhorses keep you from getting started. If you work on the ground, just lay scraps of wood underneath, providing clearance for the blade.

1. Begin by cutting all the parts to rough length. I cut them about 1 in. longer than the finished dimensions to allow for the ends to be accurately trimmed square (**PHOTO A**).

2. To square the ends, use a Speed®Square held against the sides of the stock as a cutting guide. Hold the square tight to the stock. Then hold the saw tight to the square, aligning the blade with your line of cut (**PHOTO B**). After you cut one end, turn the stock end for end. Now mark the stock to the exact length required. Align the Speed Square so that the sawblade lines up with the mark.

WORK SMART

Trim your materials an inch or two longer than the finished size first, particularly when working with long boards. This will allow a more accurate final cut to be made at each end. In addition, the materials are easier to handle and can be more easily supported.

3. Rip the supports for the lower shelves from thinner ¾-in. stock. This can be done with a handsaw or circular saw with a ripping guide. Set the guide so that the distance is 1½ in. between the guide fence and the blade. Place your wood on sawhorses or on the ground with scraps of wood to lift it (**PHOTO C**).

4. Mark the 15-degree angle on the ends of the shelf supports using a sliding T-bevel and pencil or pen (**PHOTO D**). Use a small handsaw like the dozuki saw shown in (**PHOTO E**) on the facing page to make the necessary cuts quickly and accurately. This is easier and more accurate with a handsaw than with a power saw.

MARK THE 15-DEGREE ANGLE on the narrow stock using a sliding T-bevel.

USE A CIRCULAR SAW WITH A RIPPING GUIDE to cut narrow pieces of stock from a ¾-in.-thick cedar board for the shelf supports.

USE A SMALL HANDSAW FOR CUTTING the shelf supports to length. I use a small Japanese pull saw which is more accurate and safer to use on small stock than a handheld power saw.

GUIDING CIRCULAR SAWS

Although a trained carpenter may do very precise work by eye and a steady hand, there are some simple tricks that may make even an experienced carpenter's work more accurate and efficient. Although a high level of accuracy may not seem necessary in rustic work, you will want your tables to rest firmly on the ground without rocking, and square cuts will help.

For square end cuts a Speed Square held tightly to the stock with one hand, or clamped in position with a small clamp, makes a great guide for a circular saw. Simply hold the square in place tightly to the edge of the stock, put the saw in place to start a cut, and slide the square along until the sawblade aligns with the mark for cutting length.

An aftermarket ripping guide can help make long cuts without wandering. Adjust the space between the guide and the blade to control the width of the stock. You might need to change the position of the

wood on the sawhorses as you cut to avoid cutting your sawhorses.

A clamp-on saw guide is also useful in making long ripping cuts. It is particularly useful when tapering cuts are required. Measure and allow for the width of the plate of the saw, from the edge to the blade, as you lay out your cuts.

Assemble the base

USE A CARPENTER'S SQUARE TO POSITION the shelf supports in place on the table ends. Drive the nails partway into the supports beforehand so that a single hammer blow will seat them.

DRIVE THE NAILS HOME ONCE they are through the support and started into the sides.

USE A BLOCK PLANE TO CHAMFER the edges of the sides. Moving the plane at a 45-degree angle will give the best results. Because this is a rustic table, absolute accuracy is not required.

USING ONLY NAILS, START ASSEMBLY with the alignment of the inside supports. Then add the lower shelf. Rough edges on the inside support should be sanded first. I use a carpenter's square to align the parts as the nails are driven into place. You will find it helpful to get the nails partway driven into the stock before carefully placing it in position, and then drive the nails through the support and into the sides.

1. Use a carpenter's square to align the shelf supports on the inside of the sides **(PHOTO A)**. After the nails begin to penetrate, remove the square and drive them down so the heads are flush with the surface **(PHOTO B)**.

2. Use a small plane to lightly chamfer the edges of the legs and the shelf. To plane the ends, hold the plane skewed at a 45-degree angle, not across. Planing straight across the end grain will cause

D

E

PREDRILL PILOT HOLES FOR THE NAILS that attach the sides to the shelf. Measure so that the nails will be equally spaced, then drill with a slightly smaller diameter bit than the pole barn nails.

NAIL ONE SIDE TO THE SHELF with the side supported by a cardboard box or crate. Insert the pole barn nails in the pilot holes. Position a side over one end of the shelf. Then drive the nails in tight.

F

NAIL THE OTHER SIDE TO THE OTHER END of the shelf the same way as the fist. A stack of scrap on top of the box or crate will keep it steady.

tearout (**PHOTO C**). Then plane the long edges, again holding the plane at the same angle.

3. Carefully measure and mark the locations for the pole barn nails to attach the sides to the shelf. The nails should be located about 3½ in. from each side and centered on the shelf. Then drill pilot holes for the nails (**PHOTO D**). Use a drill bit slightly smaller than the diameter of the nails, and drill from the inside surface all the way through. Drilling from the inside helps to ensure the nail hits the center of the shelf.

4. Prop the side up so that it is easy to hold the shelf in position for nailing. A crate or cardboard box will do. Insert the nails in the pilot holes and drive them partway into the table sides so that when the shelf is in position, it can be easily nailed in place (**PHOTO E**). Be careful that the shelf is tight to the support and equally spaced from the edges of the side. Then turn the parts over and follow the same procedure for nailing the other side in place (**PHOTO F**).

Add the top

THE TOP IS MADE OF TWO PIECES of 2×8 Western cedar, centered over the table ends and attached with more pole barn nails.

1. Before attaching the top, use a block plane held at an approximately 45-degree angle to chamfer the ends and sides of both top pieces. I prefer to chamfer more heavily on the bottom edges and plane more lightly on the top. Keep in mind the need to do both sides the same. I count strokes of the plane, using the same number on each part to ensure equal chamfers. Leave the center edges (where the two parts of the top will meet) only lightly chamfered (**PHOTO A**).

2. Mark the locations for the nails and drill pilot holes through the sections of the top. Use a carpenter's square to help mark the holes accurately (**PHOTO B**).

3. Mark a centerline on the sides to help with the positioning of the two top parts. Then align one half of the top, insert the nails in the pilot holes, and drive them into place (**PHOTO C**).

B

DRILL THE PILOT HOLES IN THE BOARDS for the top before attaching them to the sides. Mark the locations for the holes carefully so that the positions of the nails in the top will appear consistent.

C

ALIGN ONE BOARD FOR THE TOP where you marked the center. Also remember to space the boards equally from the ends. Then drive the nails in place.

A

USE A SMALL PLANE TO CHAMFER the edges of the tabletop pieces. Plane the end grain first, and then the long grain on the sides. By counting your strokes with the plane and duplicating the count on each edge you can get uniform results.

Variation: Coffee table and details

THERE ARE MANY WAYS TO CUSTOMIZE and personalize your rustic cedar tables. You can change the dimensions to make a coffee table or add simple details. You can mix or match the following ideas with your own.

A coffee table takes a larger top and wider base. It requires beefier shelf supports and an additional support for the top. The sides are made with two 2×8s. I use 1-in.-thick stock ripped to 1½-in.-wide strips for the shelf supports. They also serve to connect the two side pieces together.

Western cedar coffee table

By changing dimensions and adding small supports under the top, you can make a coffee table variation.

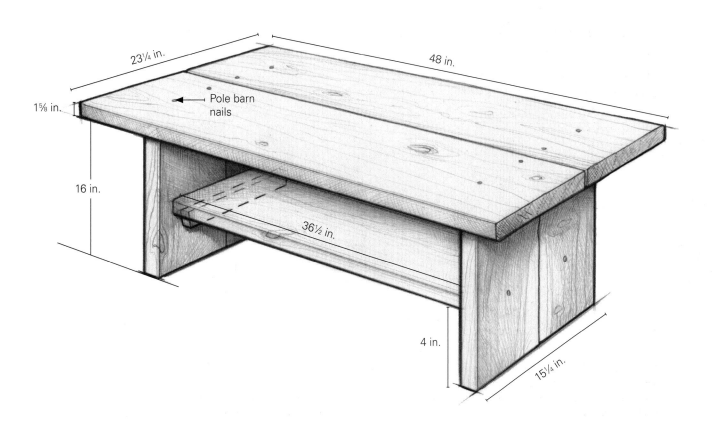

MATERIALS FOR COFFEE TABLE VARIATION

QUANTITY	PART	SIZE	NOTES
4	Sides	1⅝ in. by 7⅝ in. by 16 in.	
4	Shelf and top supports	¾ in. by 1½ in. by 10½ in.	15-degree angle each end
1	Shelf	1⅝ in. by 11⅝ in. by 36½ in.	
2	Top	1⅝ in. by 11⅝ in. by 48½ in.	from 2x12 Western red cedar
12	Pole barn nails		
16	#6 common nails		

Note: All materials from 2×8 Western red cedar unless noted.

1. Nail the shelf and top supports in place across the two pieces that make up the sides (**PHOTO A**).

2. Drill pilot holes in the sides and then secure them to the shelf with four pole barn nails. Clamping the shelf to a sawhorse will help hold it steady during assembly (**PHOTO B**).

3. Drill pilot holes in the top pieces just as for the side table. Mark the center, and align the parts on the table base. Then drive the pole barn nails in place (**PHOTO C**).

A

FOUR NAILS ARE NECESSARY TO ATTACH the shelf supports to the sides of the coffee table.

B

NAIL THE TABLE ENDS TO THE BOTTOM SHELF using the same technique as used for the side table. To keep the longer coffee table steady while nailing, I use a sawhorse instead of a crate.

C

NAIL THE COFFEE TABLE TOP boards in place the same way as for the side table.

Additional Variations

YOU CAN ADD SIMPLE DETAILS to the table for a different look. Decorative cutouts in the sides or dowels to secure the top give the table a more interesting character. You can artificially age and weather your tables with a simple treatment using common household chemicals.

Cutouts in the sides

Design a cutout for the table ends, then use a jigsaw to cut it. The diamond shape here can be laid out with a combination square With the jigsaw, either straight or curving cuts can be made. Use your imagination and see what you can come up with. You can make curving, symmetrical shapes with scissors and folded paper.

1. Cut along the marked lines with a jigsaw **(PHOTO A)**.

2. Inside cuts will take some time and greater care. The diamond squares require cutting into each corner from two directions **(PHOTO B)**.

A

HOLD THE JIGSAW STEADY WHILE making the cutouts. Make sure the board is clamped down firmly to the sawhorse as you work.

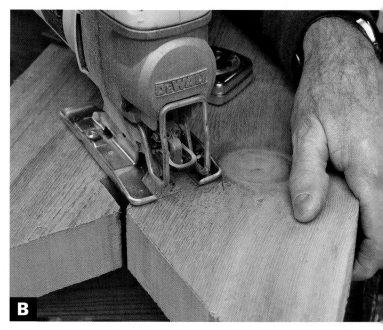

B

CUT INTO THE TIGHT CORNERS with a jigsaw, holding the board steady. Removing the bulk of waste first will make cutting the corners easier.

Shape the edge of the top

Use a circular saw set at a 45-degree angle to under-cut the edges of the top. This will make the top appear lighter.

1. Clamp a guide piece to the parts of the top to guide the saw accurately.

2. Cut the ends and then the sides, leaving the edges that align at the center of the table uncut.

USE A CIRCULAR SAW TO SHAPE the edges of the tabletop for a lighter look. By clamping a saw guide in place as shown, your cuts can be made uniform. Cut the ends first and then the sides.

Assemble your table with dowels

A

HOLD THE TABLE DOWN SECURELY with your weight as you drill holes for the dowels. I use a ⅞-in. auger bit in a ½-in. drill.

Add interest and craftsmanship to your tables by using large dowels to connect the parts.

1. First assemble the table with wood screws in place of the pole barn nails.

2. Remove the screws one at a time. Drill dowel holes with a ⅞-in.-dia. auger bit located over the screw holes. Using a ½-in. drill with a ⅞-in. auger bit produces a lot of torque. Get a good grip on the table and the drill by using your weight to hold your work steady (**PHOTO A**). A hand-powered brace will also do the job.

3. After you drill each hole, drive a ⅞-in. dowel with a rounded end in place. Add glue to the hole

B

so that it runs down the sides. Rather than damage the dowel ends by hammering on them, I use another short piece of dowel between the hammer and the dowel as it is tapped into place **(PHOTO B)**.

DRIVE DOWELS IN PLACE USING another dowel as a cushion to prevent hammer blows from marking the ends.

Weather your tables

You can give your tables an instant weathered rustic look by spraying them lightly with a diluted ebonizing solution. You can also turn them deep black by using the solution at full strength. Make the solution by taking 1 gal. of common household vinegar and dissolving a pad of 0000 steel wool in it. Put the pad into the gallon of vinegar and let it steep for 24 hours. Test the strength of the mixture by putting a cup of solution in a household plastic sprayer and lightly wetting a piece of cedar scrapwood. As the solution dries, the color will turn gray then black. Add cups of water to dilute the solution for the desired effect. Be sure to test on scraps that you have diluted the solution sufficiently before using on a finished table.

USE A STEEL WOOL AND VINEGAR SOLUTION to artificially weather your tables to a gray tone. By using the solution undiluted, you'll get black, so unless black is what you want, be careful to test on scrapwood and let the test pieces dry completely before judging your results.

Five-Board Bench

THE FIVE-BOARD bench is an American country classic. It is utterly simple in design—two legs, a top, and two stretchers. One of the great things about this project is that although there are only five basic parts, there are even fewer dimensions to keep track of. The two legs and the front and back stretchers can be handled as pairs.

When made with roughsawn lumber, this project offers the opportunity to experiment with milk paints. You can paint one color over another and then sand lightly to expose layers, giving a worn-through-the-ages look and highlighting the interesting textures from the original milling. The project is also a great way to use woods with natural edges, such as in the walnut hall table variation shown at the end of the chapter. Either variation is simple to make with hand or power tools. A few nails, screws, or dowels will offer all the strength required for many years of use.

Five-board bench

The five-board bench is a country classic made more interesting by the use of roughsawn materials and layered milk paints to highlight the textures of the wood.

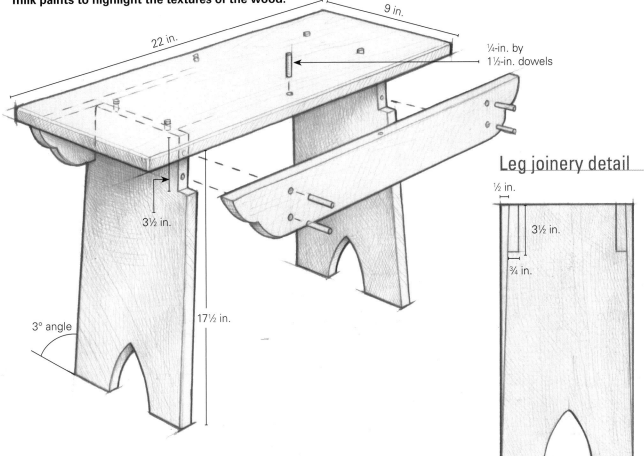

22 in.

9 in.

¼-in. by 1½-in. dowels

3½ in.

17½ in.

3° angle

Leg joinery detail

½ in.

3½ in.

¾ in.

MATERIALS FOR FIVE-BOARD BENCH

QUANTITY	PART	SIZE	MATERIAL	NOTES
1	Top	¾ in. by 9 in. by 22 in.	Yellow pine	from 2×12 Western red cedar
2	Legs	¾ in. by 9 in. by 17½ in.	Yellow pine	
2	Stretchers	¾ in. by 3½ in. by 20½ in.	Yellow pine	
16	Dowels	¼ in. dia. by 1½ in.	Birch	
8	Screws	1¼-in. #8 drywall		Temporary use during assembly
	Milk paints and clear finish	1 pt. dry mix for each color; 1 qt. clear coat		Available from The Old Fashioned Milk Paint Co., 866-350-6455, www.milkpaint.com

Prepare the stock

BEGIN BY SANDING YOUR ROUGH LUMBER
smooth to the touch. The object here is to remove splinters but leave the surface variations that resulted from the original milling of the wood.

1. Use a random-orbit sander with an 80-grit sanding disk **(PHOTO A)**. It is easiest to sand the boards before cutting them into parts.

2. Use a circular saw with a Speed square as a cutting guide to cut all the parts to length **(PHOTO B)**. The Speed square held tightly to the board with one hand provides a good guide for the saw. If uncertain of your strength, use a C-clamp to hold the square in place.

USE A RANDOM-ORBIT SANDER with coarse sanding disk to sand the splinters off, leaving the wood smooth to the touch. Sanding the whole board prior to cutting it into parts is most efficient. Sand both sides but not the edges or ends.

WORK SMART

You can make your own roughsawn lumber for these projects by using an angle grinder and coarse sanding disk. With both hands on the grinder rotate your body back and forth as you move down the board, creating the markings of a circular saw.

USE A SPEED SQUARE AND CIRCULAR SAW to cut the stock accurately into the required lengths. If you have trouble holding the Speed square in place or need two hands for the saw, use a C-clamp to secure the square to the board.

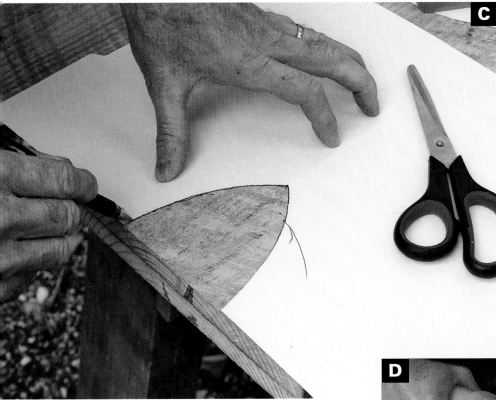

C

CLEARLY MARK THE CUTOUTS IN THE BOTTOM of the legs using a paper template. Center the cut-outs on the stock.

3. Scribe the cut-out shape in the bench ends using a folded-paper template (**PHOTO C**). Card stock or an old manila folder will be easy to trace with a pen or pencil. Simple curves or straight cuts are easiest for beginners and experienced woodworkers alike.

4. Stack the legs for sawing so that both sides will come out identical (**PHOTO D**). Clamp them securely or they may move against each other as you work. Cutting one at a time makes this less of a concern.

Clamp your parts together in a stack to simplify the steps when cutting or shaping. But be careful: If you mess up, you will mess up both.

JIGSAW THE STACKED BENCH ENDS. Make certain they are clamped securely so they don't shift as you make your cut.

Taper and fit the legs

MARK THE TAPER ON THE LEGS. Align your straight edge ½ in. in from top with the bottom corner. Mark both sides.

STACK AND CLAMP YOUR BENCH LEGS together on the sawhorse and use a circular saw to cut the tapers. You can use a clamped guide for this, or cut freehand, just watching and following the line as you cut.

TAPERING THE LEGS MAKES THE BENCH appear less top heavy while still providing a wide base for stability.

1. Clamp the two legs together and lay out the taper. I start ½ in. in from the top edge, and mark a line to the bottom corner **(PHOTO A)**.

2. Cut the taper with a circular saw, following the line by eye **(PHOTO B)**.

3. Lightly bump the edges with an angle grinder and sanding disc to add texture. To achieve a random surface, vary the angle and position, never staying long in one spot. You could choose to sand the edges smooth, but grinding fits with the other rough surfaces and will create a more rustic look when you apply milk paint. You can do this without an angle grinder by using a rasp or a very coarse sanding block **(PHOTO C)**.

USE AN ANGLE GRINDER AND COARSE sanding disk to roughen the edges of the legs. If you don't have an angle grinder, use a rasp, taking random strokes across the edge. Clamp the pieces together on the sawhorse so that two edges can be done at one time.

D

MARK THE LEGS FOR CUTTING the joint
for the front and back stretchers. Clamp the
parts together standing vertically on the sawhorse for both measuring and marking.

E

F

USE A HANDSAW
TO MAKE THE VER-
TICAL CUTS in the
bench ends for attach-
ing the front and back
stretchers. Keep the
sawblade level at the
end of the cut so that
you cut to the same
depth on both parts.

TURN THE LEGS ON
THEIR SIDES to fin-
ish cutting the joints
for the stretchers.

4. Mark the cutouts for the front and back
stretchers to fit. Because the edges have been
tapered, align the square from the top of the
legs **(PHOTO D)**.

5. Cut along the marked lines with a handsaw.
I use a Japanese pull saw. However, an American or
European-style handsaw or dovetail saw will work
well **(PHOTO E)**. Clamp the boards securely to your
sawhorse, and with the legs clamped together both
parts can be cut at the same time.

6. Turn the parts on their side to finish the
cutouts **(PHOTO F)**.

WORK
SMART

Cutting folded paper makes more
accurate symmetrical patterns than
marking individual papers. Cardstock
or an old manila folder work best.
Fold the paper in half, and then cut
through both layers at the same
time. The fold can be used to control
the position of the template on
the stock as you mark its shape in
pencil or pen.

Make the stretchers

THE STRETCHERS CONNECTING THE TWO LEGS have a decorative feature on their ends.

1. Use a circular saw and ripping guide to cut the stretchers to width. For accuracy, it will help to rip both parts at the same time **(PHOTO A)**. To avoid leaving cut marks in your sawhorses, you will need to keep adjusting the position of the material and saw during the cut.

RIP STOCK FOR THE FRONT AND BACK stretchers with a circular saw and ripping guide. I set the guide so that the fence and blade are 3 in. apart. Cut a piece long enough for both the front and back, rather than trying to rip short stock.

MARK OUT THE DESIGN ON THE STRETCHER ENDS with a card-stock template. Use scissors and card stock to design the stretcher ends.

2. Mark the decorative curves on the ends of the stretchers using a folded card-stock template. Fold a piece of paper in half, mark the dimensions of the stock on it, and then cut out the shape. The fold at the top edge of the template helps to align it on the face of the stock **(PHOTO B)**. Use card stock for the most accurate results in tracing, because thin paper can deflect as you trace. You may find as I have that it is often easier to design with scissors than with a pencil, and with scissors if you don't like the design you've come up with, cut again.

3. Use a jigsaw to cut the curves. By clamping the two stretchers together, they can be cut at the same time **(PHOTO C)**.

STACK AND CLAMP THE STRETCHERS TOGETHER, then use a jigsaw to cut their shape.

Assembly

THE SIMPLE APPROACH AT THIS POINT is to use nails to secure the stretchers to the legs. But I chose to use dowels instead. This requires first holding the parts together with screws, then removing the screws one at a time, enlarging the screw holes to ¼ in., and then driving dowels in place. For strength and stability, I angle the bench legs slightly outward at the bottom. Marking that angle on the stretchers is the first step in assembly.

1. Before assembly, use a block plane or sandpaper wrapped on a block of wood to soften the edges of all the parts. You are not looking for a flawless finish, but one that shows varying surface textures (**PHOTO A**). A rasp also works well for softening the edges of the curved surfaces (**PHOTO B**). It's a good rule to sand before assembling all areas that would be more difficult to sand afterward.

B

USE A RASP TO FINISH THE EDGES of the front and back stretchers. The object here is to remove the jigsaw marks and gently round the edges.

C

USE A SLIDING T-BEVEL TO MARK where the legs fit the stretchers. By attaching the legs at a slight angle you gain stability.

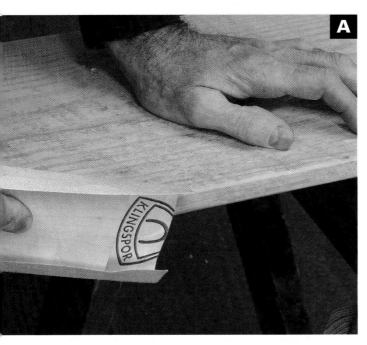

A

A SANDING BLOCK WORKS TO SOFTEN the edges of the top. The object isn't to have a perfect edge but rather one that feels soft to the touch and prevents splinters.

2. Use a sliding T-bevel and pencil or pen to mark the locations and angles for the legs on the front and back stretchers (**PHOTO C**).

3. Place the bench parts upside down on a firm surface. Align the parts on the marks and use clamps to hold everything together.

D

USE A DRILL TO MAKE PILOT HOLES for tempo-
rary screws to hold the legs to the stretchers.

E

REPLACE THE SCREWS WITH ¼-IN. DOWELS,
drilling out each screw hole. Replace only one screw at a
time, leaving the rest to hold the bench ends in place and
at right angles to the stretchers.

F

KEEP THE BENCH CLAMPED TOGETHER on a flat
surface as the glue dries after installing the dowels.

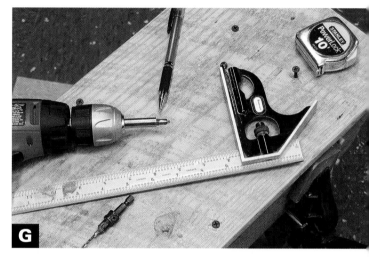

G

CAREFULLY MARK AND DRILL FOR INSTALLING
the top board of the bench. I begin by drilling pilot holes.
When all the screws are in place, I remove them one at a
time, drilling and gluing a ¼-in. dowel in place before moving on to the next.

4. Drill pilot holes with a ⅛-in. bit. Then drive
the screws in place, temporarily securing the parts
together **(PHOTO D)**.

5. Cut the dowels about ⁵⁄₁₆ in. longer than the
depth of the holes. Sand the ends. Then, one at a
time, remove the screws, drill the holes larger with
a ¼-in. bit, and glue each dowel in place. If using

polyurethane glue, wipe the dowel with a damp
cloth before driving it in place **(PHOTO E)**.

6. Keep the clamps in place until the polyurethane
glue is fully dried **(PHOTO F)**.

7. For attaching the top, use the same strategy in
adding then removing screws and replacing them
with dowels **(PHOTO G)**.

With layers of color, you can add a great deal of interest to rustic work. You can create a piece that appears very old and worn, and highlight subtle variations in texture, creating timeless beauty from rather uninteresting materials. One of the best ways to add color is the use of milk paints. Milk paint is a traditional nontoxic, long-wearing colorant for wood that you mix from a dry formula. The milk paint I use is available in many craft and art supply stores and is manufactured by The Old Fashioned Milk Paint Co.

One of the advantages of milk paint is that it can be sanded easily without loading the sandpaper. You can sand easily through layers of different colors—

two, three, or even more—highlighting texture and adding the playful use of color to your work.

Working with colors may seem risky for most woodworkers, but that risk is minimized and the use of color becomes fun when you've tested your results before applying to your near-finished work. So first make a test board of the same material that you will use for your layered milk paint finish. Sand and prepare the material just the way you will in the real project. Experiment with different colors and arrangements of layers. Wait for each coat to dry before the next one is applied. Then experiment with light sanding to reveal the color (or colors) underneath.

Apply the finish

APPLY THE FIRST COAT OF MILK PAINT directly to the raw wood. Be careful to work the paint into the recesses in the roughsawn material.

APPLY THE SECOND COLOR over the first after it has dried.

USE SANDPAPER TO LIGHTLY sand through the second coat, revealing the color beneath. You can sand more heavily in areas that would normally receive the most wear, making the piece look old.

AFTER EXPERIMENTING ON SCRAPWOOD with a variety of color combinations, I decided to paint the first coat with "Barn Red," to be followed by "Lexington Green." Both of these colors are available from The Old Fashioned Milk Paint Company, a supplier of milk paints for artists (see the materials chart on p. 17).

1. Mix the red milk paint with water in the proportions stated in the instructions (50–50 by volume). Then brush it on. No primer is required. You will need to work the paint into the rough texture (**PHOTO A**).

2. Apply the second coat directly over the first. No sanding is required. Again, be careful to cover the deeper recesses in the grain and texture with each coat (**PHOTO B**).

3. Use 220- or 240-grit sandpaper to lightly sand the second coat after it dries (**PHOTO C**). Depending on how long and how hard you sand, you'll reveal a varying amount of the undercoat, adding contrast and accentuating the texture of the wood.

APPLY A CLEAR COAT ACRYLIC FINISH to protect the colors and seal the finish from additional wear.

4. When you achieve the look you like, wipe down the bench with a soft cloth or blow it with a compressor to remove sanding dust. Then give the bench a clear coat to protect and preserve the milk paint finish (**PHOTO D**).

Variation:
Natural-edged hall table

THE SIMPLE DESIGN OF THE FIVE-BOARD BENCH can be adapted to other styles of rustic furniture. Despite its highly sanded finish, this walnut hall table derives its rustic character from the natural edges. Only the bark has been removed.

This bench is made entirely from two matching walnut boards. In addition to the five boards of the basic bench, I added two more: one to make a shelf at the bottom and a second stabilizing the bottom back. However, the furniture you make will depend on the length and width of the material available.

Walnut hall table

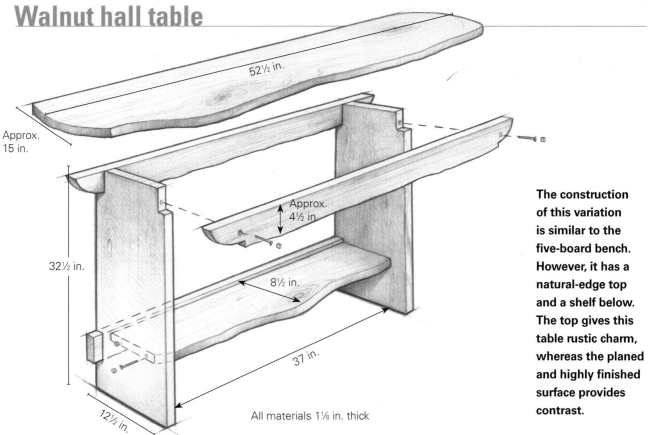

52½ in.

Approx. 15 in.

Approx. 4½ in.

32½ in.

8½ in.

37 in.

12½ in.

All materials 1⅛ in. thick

The construction of this variation is similar to the five-board bench. However, it has a natural-edge top and a shelf below. The top gives this table rustic charm, whereas the planed and highly finished surface provides contrast.

Prepare the stock

RIP THE PARTS TO WIDTH with a guide.

ROUGH CUT YOUR PIECES TO LENGTH by eye with a circular saw. Leave each piece about 1 in. longer than the finished length.

USE A SCRUB PLANE TO LEVEL the surface of the roughsawn pieces that are too wide for your planer.

1. First rough cut all the parts from the larger board, each an inch or more longer than finished dimensions **(PHOTO A)**.

2. Use a guide to make straight cuts for the back side of the tabletop and for the back edges of the legs **(PHOTO B)**. A commercially made sawing guide or just a thin and straight piece of plywood wide enough to keep from flexing will both work well.

3. I used a scrub plane to surface the top roughly **(PHOTO C)**, then smoothed it with a smoothing plane and orbital sander **(PHOTO D)**. I did this because the top was the only board too wide to pass through the planer.

4. Because the legs, bottom shelf, and stretchers were narrow enough to pass through my 12½-in. planer, I used it to surface them to 1⅛ in. thick **(PHOTO E)**.

A SMOOTH-ING PLANE will make your level surface smooth.

USE A PLANER to surface those parts narrow enough to pass through.

Taper and fit the legs

1. Taper the edge of the legs using a circular saw with a ripping guide clamped at a right angle. This can also be done freehand as for the five-board bench. But I wanted a smooth and straight edge rather than a textured edge **(PHOTO A)**.

2. Use a smoothing plane to remove the saw marks on the edge **(PHOTO B)**.

3. Carefully mark the locations of the joints for the front and back stretchers to fit in the legs. Then cut the joints using the same technique shown for the five-board bench on p. 21 **(PHOTO C)**.

USE A HANDPLANE TO SMOOTH the sawn edges prior to sanding.

CUT THE TAPER ON THE LEGS with a circular saw and ripping guide.

USE A HANDSAW TO CUT THE JOINTS in the legs for the stretchers.

Make the stretchers and top

USE PAPER TEMPLATES TO LAY OUT the curved ends of the front and back stretchers.

B

CUT THE CURVED ENDS of the stretchers with a jigsaw.

PLANT YOUR ELBOW FIRMLY and swing your arm, pen-in-hand, to convey the natural geometry of your body to the design of your work.

CUT THE ENDS OF THE TOP BOARDS with the jigsaw blade angled about 5 degrees.

1. Using a paper template, mark out the design at the end of the stretchers (**PHOTO A**). Cut the shape with a jigsaw (**PHOTO B**).

2. Use the natural pivot of your arm at the elbow to design the curved shape of the ends of the tabletop (**PHOTO C**).

3. Use a jigsaw with the blade tilted at about 5 degrees to follow the line and cut the top to shape (**PHOTO D**). The ends of this table need not be perfectly symmetrical, so the same technique can be used on both ends.

Assembly and finishing

1. Attach the stretchers to the legs using countersunk wood screws (**PHOTO A**).

2. Hide the screws with raised walnut plugs (**PHOTO B**). Put a bit of glue on the edges of the hole and use a short dowel to cushion between the plug and the face of the hammer. Screws from two directions lock the joint.

3. Use pocket-hole screws to attach the base to the top from underneath (**PHOTO C**).

4. Sand all the parts to 320 grit with the exception of the natural edges, then apply three coats of clear Danish oil.

A

COUNTERSINK WOOD SCREWS to secure the joints. The screws will be hidden with raised walnut plugs.

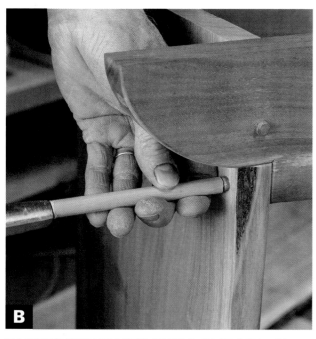

B

HAMMER THE WALNUT PLUGS IN PLACE with a short dowel as a nail set to avoid damaging them.

C

USE A KREG® POCKET-HOLE JIG to drill recesses in the legs and front and back stretchers for securing the top to the base.

Stick, Twig, and Branch Tables

THESE SMALL TABLES, made with fresh-cut sycamore twigs and branches, are perfect in an entry hall . . . a place to put a hat, purse, or keys. They're made from materials harvested straight from the forest. A piece of ½-in. plywood provides the foundation for a richly textured random mosaic on top. The legs are 1½-in.-thick stock cut from a sapling.

Although this table is made of sycamore, other woods will work as well or even better. For example, willow has straight flexible branches that are easier to arrange in a more uniform pattern. You will notice that my pattern is not completely random. I liked the way the twigs looked when I cut at an angle on the ends. I arranged them so that the ends formed a consistent pattern around the perimeter of the top.

Square stick, twig, and branch table

This branch and twig table is made from freshly harvested sycamore. The random mosaic pattern on the top is made of short pieces of branch nailed to a plywood base. This simple construction technique can be used on tables of any size and shape, bringing forest textures into your home. Use pruning shears to cut the twigs to fit. The stretchers strengthening the legs are added on the outside using an air nailer to secure them in place.

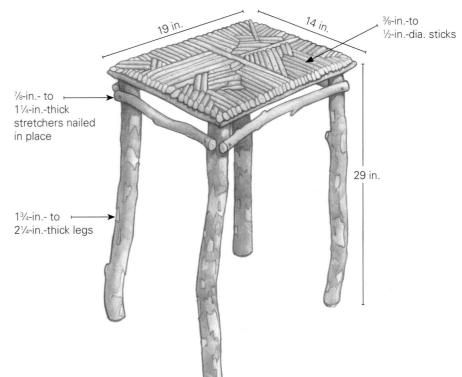

19 in.

14 in.

⅜-in.-to ½-in.-dia. sticks

⅞-in.- to 1¼-in.-thick stretchers nailed in place

1¾-in.- to 2¼-in.-thick legs

29 in.

MATERIALS FOR STICK, TWIG, AND BRANCH TABLE

QUANTITY	PART	SIZE	MATERIAL	NOTES
1	Top	½ in. by 13 in. by 18 in.	Baltic birch plywood	
4	Legs	1¾ in. to 2¼ in. by 28 in.	Sycamore or other fresh-cut hardwood	Rough cut 1 in. to 2 in. longer
2	Apron	⅞ in. to 1⅛ in. by 17½ in.	Sycamore or other fresh-cut hardwood	Rough cut 1 in. to 2 in. longer
2	Apron	⅞ in. to 1⅛ in. by 13 in.	Sycamore or other fresh-cut hardwood	Rough cut 1 in. to 2 in. longer
60 ft.	Twigs	⅜ in. to ½ in. dia.	Sycamore or other fresh-cut hardwood	
4	Screws	3-in. #8 porch and deck		
200	Nails	1³⁄₁₆-in. brad		
12	Nails	2-in. brad		
4	Furniture glides	⅞ in.		Available from www. allglides.com, stock number SG87

Cut and attach the legs

USE A HANDSAW TO CUT BRANCHES or a slender sapling to length for the legs.

SCREW THE LEGS IN PLACE with the top clamped to sawhorses. They support the legs as you screw them in place.

THE LEGS ON THIS SIMPLE TABLE get their strength both from the screws driven through the plywood top and from the stretchers nailed to the outside.

1. Cut the plywood top to size. This can be done on a tablesaw, with a handheld circular saw, or even with a handsaw.

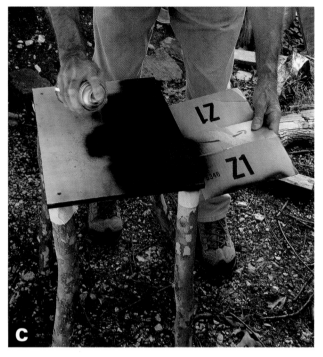

SPRAY PAINT THE PLYWOOD TOP. Use a piece of cardboard to shield the legs from overspray. Also put masking tape around the tops of each leg for extra protection from the paint.

2. Use a handsaw to cut the legs to length. I cut the four legs for this table from a single sapling. The slight variation in thickness makes very little difference in the finished work **(PHOTO A)**.

3. Use screws to attach the tabletop to the legs. Clamping the top to a sawhorse will help you to hold the legs tight while you drive the screws in place **(PHOTO B)**. I use 2½-in.-long exterior deck screws to secure the legs.

4. Paint the plywood top using black spray paint. The black paint will make the top nearly invisible if seen through the sticks. Use masking tape and a piece of cardboard to protect the legs as you paint **(PHOTO C)**.

Create the top mosaic

I USE BRANCHES TO COMPLETELY COVER the plywood top and edges. On this table, it is OK if the top isn't perfectly smooth. I try to secure the pieces together tightly to minimize the space between. If you don't have a nail gun, you can use a hammer, but you will need to drill pilot holes to avoid splitting. Fresh-cut branches will be easier to cut, more flexible to bend into shape, and less likely to split as they are nailed.

1. Carefully trim the branches to fit using pruning shears **(PHOTO A)**. If your branches are irregular in shape, you can make things easier by cutting them in short pieces laid end to end.

2. Cover the edges with thin branches. I cut miters where the branches meet in the corners and then use a nail gun to attach the branches in place. Pay close attention to the placement of your fingers to avoid accidents. They should be at least a nail's length from the tip of the gun at all times **(PHOTO B)**.

NAIL THE BRANCHES IN PLACE with an air gun. I use 1³⁄₁₆-in.-long nails and am careful to keep my fingers at least a nail's distance from the nailing point.

USE PRUNING SHEARS TO CUT THE ENDS of the branches. A final trimming cut following a rough cut will give a smoother surface.

WORK SMART

You will find that freshly cut "green" material will be much easier to work with than dry wood. When wood dries, the cell walls harden, making it harder to cut and harder to bend or nail.

BEGIN CREATING A RANDOM MOSAIC by nailing down longer twig stock first. Carefully angle the nail gun so that the nails don't pass through the underside of the plywood.

3. On the top, place branches in a random pattern, first dividing the top into sections, then filling the sections by adding one piece after another. I cut the ends at the angles required to fit tight to adjoining stock. Use the nail gun at an angle so the nails won't poke through the other side **(PHOTO C)**. Check where your fingers are with each shot to avoid accidents.

4. Gradually fill the space on the top, stick by stick. I arrange pieces so that I get a pattern of chamfered tips around the perimeter of the top. This gives a more uniform look to the edge, so it looks more consistent from a variety of angles, and I like the pattern it creates **(PHOTO D)**.

Two cuts are better than one. Cut twigs just a bit long and then make a second cut. The second, removing just a small amount of material, will give a cleaner cut and a more refined and accurate look to the finished table.

5. Cut pieces to fill the corners, too. There is no exact pattern to follow. Just cut and fill until the entire top is covered **(PHOTO E)**. Even very short pieces can be used. Use the tip of the nail gun to hold them as you nail them in place.

NAIL ADDITIONAL PIECES BETWEEN the longer twigs, varying your pattern.

SHORT PIECES CAN BE NAILED through the end as you fill in the corners. Note how all the pieces are oriented with the ends to the outside, creating a uniform pattern at the table edge.

Add stretchers to strengthen the legs

STRENGTHEN THE LEGS ON THE TABLE by adding stretchers to the outside. These parts are required to make the table stable and strong. I use branches slightly thicker than the material for the mosaic pattern. Nails are sufficient to hold them securely in place. If you don't have a nail gun avail-able, use screws so you can avoid hammering on the legs, as that could weaken the joints rather than make them strong. Choose your nail length by adding the thicknesses of the leg and the stretcher together. The nail should be just shorter than that length.

1. Cut the branches to a length equal to the width and depth of the table. I angle the cuts slightly so they don't stick out too far at the corners.

2. Use the nail gun to attach the stretchers to the legs. Use nails long enough to pass through the stretchers and well into the legs. I use two or more nails to attach each end and angle each nail differently to provide additional resistance to pulling out **(PHOTO A)**.

ATTACH STRETCHER STOCK TO THE OUTSIDES of the table legs with longer nails. Use two or more nails from various angles through the stretcher and into the legs.

Variation: Round table

ROUND TABLES ARE PARTICULARLY APPEALING. Tables of this type can be made in any size or shape. This one was made with green walnut sticks and twigs. Putting the twig edge on the round top requires that you use material that is fresh cut and flexible in order to bend it to shape without breaking.

Round stick, twig, and branch table

This walnut round variation requires fresh-cut or "green" material to make the bends around the plywood disk. This small table would be great as an end table or could be made oval or rectangular to serve as a coffee table.

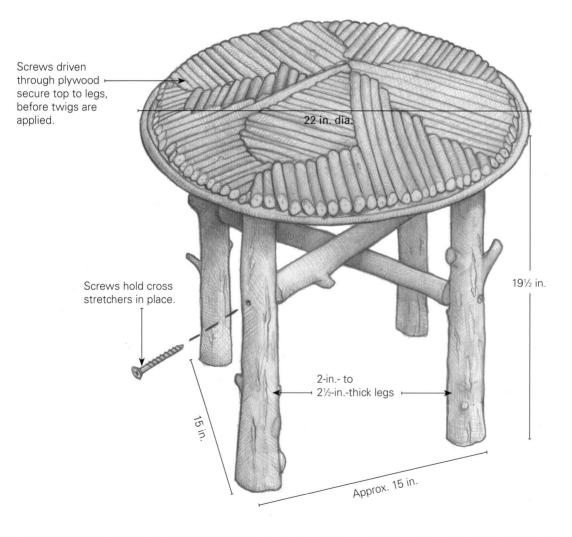

Screws driven through plywood secure top to legs, before twigs are applied.

22 in. dia.

Screws hold cross stretchers in place.

19½ in.

2-in.- to 2½-in.-thick legs

15 in.

Approx. 15 in.

MATERIALS FOR ROUND VARIATION

QUANTITY	PART	SIZE	MATERIAL	NOTES
1	Top	½ in. by 21 in. dia.	Baltic birch plywood	
4	Legs	2 in. to 2¼ in. by 18½ in.	Walnut or other fresh-cut hardwood	
2	Stretchers	1 in. to 1⅛ in. by 15 in. approximate length	Walnut or other fresh-cut hardwood	Determine final length by measuring between legs
90 ft.	Twigs	⅜ in. to ½ in. dia.	Walnut or other fresh-cut hardwood	
8	Screws	3-in. #8 porch and deck		
1	Screw	1¼-in. #6		
300	Nails	1³⁄₁₆-in. brad		
4	Furniture glides	⅞ in.		Available from www.allglides.com, stock number SG87

Cut the top to shape

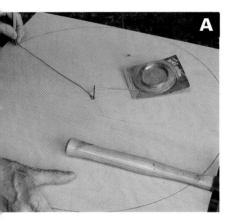

MARK THE CIRCUM-FERENCE OF THE TABLETOP using a string or wire and a pencil and nail. Loops at each end of the wire control the radius of the circle.

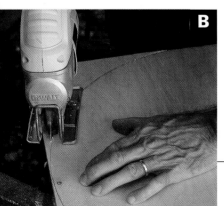

USE A JIGSAW TO CUT THE CIRCLE, following your layout line carefully.

The round top of this table is ½-in. Baltic birch plywood. I use wire, a nail, and a pencil as a compass for marking the diameter of the table on the wood.

1. Cut the Baltic birch plywood to a square shape just slightly larger than the diameter of the tabletop.

2. Find the center of the tabletop by marking from corner to corner. Then drive a nail partway into the wood at the center to form a pivot point for the compass. I used a piece of picture-hanging wire, with one end over the nail and the other looped around a pencil, for a compass. String could be used for this, but string stretches so is not as accurate **(PHOTO A)**.

3. Cut the top to shape using a jigsaw. Follow the line you have marked **(PHOTO B)**.

Make the base

SAW THE LEGS TO LENGTH USING A HANDSAW. Despite some minor variations in diameter, I was able to cut all four legs from a single small sapling.

B

USE PORCH AND DECK SCREWS TO ATTACH the plywood top to the legs. I drive the screw partway through the top, then center the leg against the protruding screw and finish driving the screw into the leg.

Cross-stretchers forming an X make the legs in this variation stronger. For the sake of variety, you can use either this technique or the one for the square table.

1. Cut the legs to length from 2-in.-dia. to 2½-in.-dia. branches. These may be straight or crooked. Straight ones are easier to install, whereas crooked branches may be more interesting in the finished table **(PHOTO A)**.

2. Drive screws through the plywood to attach the legs. Try to space them uniformly and an equal distance from the edge **(PHOTO B)**.

3. Cut thinner branch stock to use as stretchers between the legs. Measure the distance between opposite legs and cut the stock to that length. Use countersunk wood screws to hold the first stretcher in place (**PHOTO C**).

4. Before installing the second cross stretcher, carve a small notch where the two intersect. This will allow the cross stretchers to be screwed securely to each other (**PHOTO D**).

5. After screwing the second stretcher to the legs, screw the stretchers together from underneath. Drill a pilot hole and select the length of the screw so that it won't go all the way through both pieces of stock. This way, the screw won't be visible (**PHOTO E**).

A NOTCH IN ONE STRETCHER WILL INCREASE the strength of the joint between them. Use a knife to cut the notch where the stretchers intersect.

PREDRILL, COUNTERSINK, AND SCREW THE LEGS to the cross stretchers. The ⅜-in. countersunk hole is just the right size for a dowel plug.

DRILL AND COUNTERSINK A PILOT HOLE at the intersection of the two cross stretchers from underneath. Screw them together.

Finish the top

Making a mosaic pattern on a round top is very much like making a patterned top on a square or rectangular one, except that particularly flexible material is required for applying twigs to cover the edge.

1. Use black or dark spray paint to cover the plywood top. I use a piece of cardboard as a mask to protect the legs from overspray **(PHOTO A)**.

2. Use a nail gun to apply the edge stock. I use a clamp to help hold it tight to the plywood and follow around the perimeter driving nails in place. Move the clamp as necessary to hold the twig material in place while you nail **(PHOTO B)**. Keep your fingers out of the direct line of fire and wear safety glasses to keep your eyes safe in the event that a nail misses and ricochets. Bending the material before nailing can help.

A

PAINT THE TABLETOP BLACK. I use piece of cardboard to prevent overspray.

B

USE A NAIL GUN TO ATTACH SLENDER stock to cover the edge of the plywood. A pipe clamp is useful to hold the stock tightly in place while you nail. This job can be done with a hammer and conventional nails, too.

C

AS YOU SPLICE PIECES ON THE EDGE, cut them at a diagonal so they overlap slightly. This will help to secure them tightly to the edge.

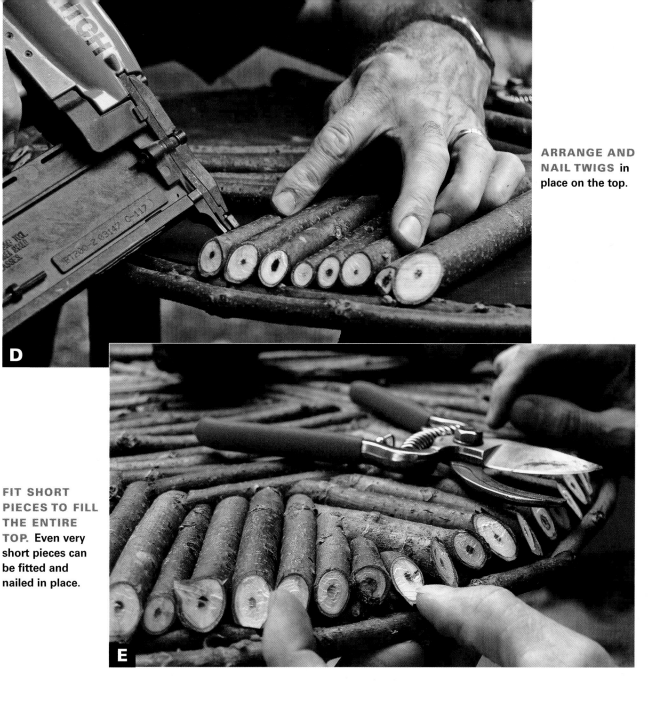

ARRANGE AND NAIL TWIGS in place on the top.

FIT SHORT PIECES TO FILL THE ENTIRE TOP. Even very short pieces can be fitted and nailed in place.

3. Cut the twig stock at an angle where splices need to be made (**PHOTO C**).

4. Design the mosaic by laying some long pieces in first and then filling the spaces. My only nod to order and regularity is to have twigs pointing outward at all points around the circumference. I also cut the twigs at an angle sloping down toward the table edge (**PHOTO D**).

5. Keep adding pieces of varying lengths as required. There is no special pattern to follow in this, and random patterns are easier to achieve (**PHOTO E**).

6. The finished table can be coated with Danish oil or left natural. The Danish oil will darken the wood and provide protection from normal wear. I use a spray bottle to apply the finish and then a dry cloth to wipe off excess. This should be done before the oil starts to get sticky, usually 15 to 20 minutes after application.

Slab
Bench

FOR OVER 30 YEARS I've collected pieces of wood that are too useless to use and too beautiful to throw out. Sometimes the outermost board from milling a log is wane on one face but may have beautiful figure on the other. It's not big enough

for sawing lumber larger than Popsicle® sticks, but you can turn it into a slab table or bench: A slab of wood, four legs, and wedged mortise-and-tenon joints is a simple and timeless design.

Sawmills and even portable Wood-Mizer® sawmills are good

sources for that first cut of the log. In addition, I've found it useful to keep an eye open for the activities of tree trimmers in my town. They often leave things when they are finished, like the stump used later in this chapter.

Slab bench

This very simple piece of furniture is made from the first cut of a maple log, wood that often goes to waste at sawmills. The octagonal ash legs are attached to the top with mortise-and-tenon joints secured with walnut wedges. As an alternative design, natural limbs could be used to form the legs.

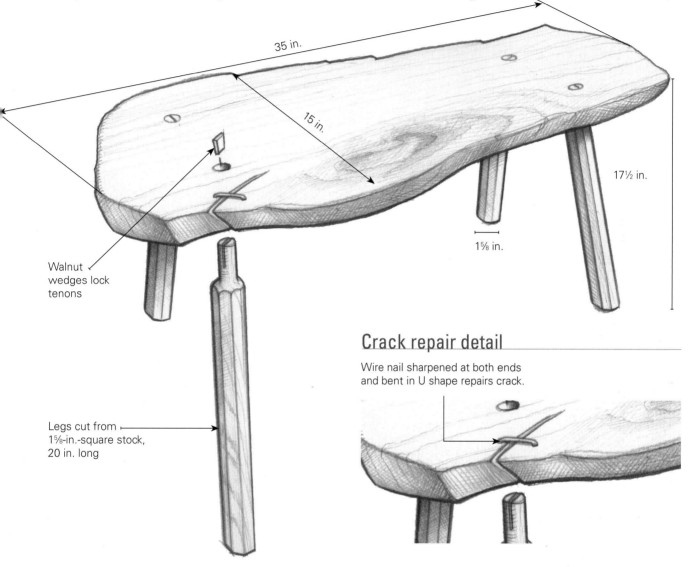

35 in.

15 in.

17½ in.

1⅝ in.

Walnut wedges lock tenons

Legs cut from 1⅝-in.-square stock, 20 in. long

Crack repair detail

Wire nail sharpened at both ends and bent in U shape repairs crack.

MATERIALS FOR SLAB BENCH

QUANTITY	PART	SIZE	NOTES
1	Slab	35 in. by 15 in.	
4	Legs	1⅝ in. by 20 in.	
4	Wedges	1 in. by 3 in. approx.	
4	Furniture glides	⅞ in.	Available from www.allglides.com, stock number SG87

Cut the slab to size

USE A CHAINSAW TO CUT your piece of slab from the surrounding stock. Prop the stock up on blocks of wood to keep the sawblade from hitting the ground. Here I cut at a slight angle to create an undercut on the ends.

USE A CHAINSAW TO CUT your slab to the desired length. As no two slabs are the same, I can give no instruction on size or shape, just guidelines. Look for sections of wood that appear sound. Avoid severe or deep cracks. There is no exact formula for the perfect shape. I made the chainsaw cuts in this piece of spalted maple at an angle toward the underside (PHOTO A), but I could have chosen for equally good reasons to square the cut or angle it the other way. These choices make the work very personal, reflecting your own judgment, experimentation, and taste. I chose to cut from the widest point and to capture an area of beautiful figure and spalting on the other side.

Surface the top

I USE A VARIETY OF GRINDING AND SANDING devices to reveal the beauty of the wood on the top surface. Because I'm not overly concerned with making it perfectly flat, I start with an angle grinder and 40-grit sanding disk to remove material quickly. You could also use a scrub plane to start, choosing to rely completely on hand tools. Watch your work carefully as you remove the coarse saw marks on the surface. Don't linger, allowing the disk to dig deep (PHOTO B). Next I use a

USE AN ANGLE GRINDER AND COARSE sanding disk to begin smoothing the surface.

C

WORK YOUR WAY THROUGH THE SANDING grits with a random-orbit sander up through 320 grit and expose the hidden beauty of the grain.

random-orbit sander, starting with 80 grit and then in sequence through 100, 120, 180, and 220. Finally I switch to a half-sheet orbital sander (or paper and a sanding block) with 320-grit paper for the final sanding. I could have done all the sanding with the random-orbit sander, but feel I get a better finish with the half-sheet sander or by hand **(PHOTO C).**

WORK SMART

Rustic furniture, whether a table or bench, need not be perfectly flat or level. But the character of wood grain is made more interesting and visible if you have carefully removed machine and sanding marks. Sanding with a careful sequence of grits from coarse to fine will bring dull wood to life and give it greater depth and luster.

Shape the edges

THERE ARE A VARIETY OF WAYS to do this step. A small drawknife or spokeshave will work well, though a rasp or a sanding block will work to equal effect. The object is to soften the edges, making them less brittle and less sharp. You will find that paying attention to the direction of the wood grain will help to avoid digging in or chipping out. To get the best results, pull the drawknife in the direction the grain exits the wood. Going against the grain will cause the tool to dig in and remove chunks rather than cut fine shavings **(PHOTO D).**

I USE A DRAWKNIFE TO SHAPE and finish the edges of the slab. As much as possible, pull with the grain, not against it.

D

Make and shape the legs

TO ATTAIN AN EVEN MORE RUSTIC LOOK
I could have used natural branches for legs. Instead
I chose 2-in.-thick ash and milled it into octagons.

1. On the tablesaw, cut the leg stock to a uniform
square shape.

2. Bevel the edges at 45 degrees to make eight-
sided legs **(PHOTO A)**.

3. Cut the legs to uniform length. I use a sled and
stop block on the tablesaw **(PHOTO B)**. Square up
one end, then slide that end against the stop block
and cut the other.

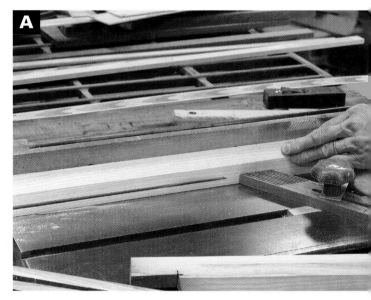

**USE A TABLESAW
AND RIPPING
FENCE** to size the
2-in.-thick stock
required to make the
legs. Tilt the blade to
45 degrees and cut
away the corners.

**USE A CROSSCUT
SLED AND STOP
BLOCK** to cut the
legs to the required
length. Be certain to
square one end first.

Drill the mortises

THE ANGLE YOU DRILL THE MORTISES will determine the look of the piece. So use your visualization skills before you begin, or do a sketch and experiment with various angles. When you drill the mortises, if you want your legs to flare out slightly, adjust the angle that you hold the drill. If you want the legs to be straight, be careful that you hold the drill as vertical as you possibly can.

Fit a dowel as long as the leg in the first mortise you drill. It will help you align your stance, posture, and grip for the next mortise.

If you've ever drilled all the way through a board, you know that drills break through the underside, tearing out chunks and leaving a mess. To avoid this, clamp a backing piece on the back of the board before you drill so that the drill cuts through cleanly. I used a piece of scrap ¾-in. plywood held in place with a large handscrew.

Use a 1-in. drill and Forstner bit to drill the holes for the mortises. Don't overwork the drill: You can make it go easier if you pull the bit out now and then to remove sawdust buildup in the mortise.

DRILL THE MORTISES THROUGH THE SLAB into a waste block clamped to the face of the slab. The block prevents tearout as the bit exits the wood.

WORK SMART

When drilling holes clear through stock, clamp a scrap tightly in place where the bit will exit. This is in order to prevent tearout where the drill bit exits the stock. Throughout the drilling operation the bit works its way in solid wood.

Cut the tenons on the legs

CLAMP EACH LEG TO A SAWHORSE and check that it's level before cutting the tenon. This allows you to take advantage of the level built into the Veritas tenon cutter.

HOLD YOUR BODY STEADY AS YOU cut the tenon. Carefully guide the tenon cutter onto the end of the stock. Line the drill and tenon cutter up visually from above and make use of the level for horizontal adjustment.

I USE A 1-IN. VERITAS® TENON CUTTER to cut tenons on the ends of the legs. This jig works whether the legs are dimensioned stock or natural tree limbs. The tenon cutter makes fitting the legs to the slab easy. You may want to do a test piece with scrapwood first and adjust the blade if needed. The tenon cutter has a built-in level that helps you position the tool level to the stock.

1. Clamp the leg stock to a sawhorse.

2. Place a small level on top of the leg. Adjust the leg until the bubble centers in the glass **(PHOTO A)**. Then make sure the clamps are locked down tight.

3. Check the bubble in the level of the tenoner as you align the drill with the leg, watching from above. Hold your position steady as you feed the tenoner over the end of the leg **(PHOTO B)**. Do this same operation for each leg.

Assemble the legs and slab

TO LOCK THE LEGS IN THE SLAB, I wedge the tenons. The wedges of a contrasting color are driven into place after the legs are inserted in the mortises. The wedges expand the tenons, tightening them in place. I chose contrasting walnut wedges to highlight handwork and individual craftsmanship.

1. Clamp the legs one at a time to the sawhorse and cut a kerf partway down the length of the tenon with a handsaw **(PHOTO A)**. To avoid splitting the leg and to maintain full strength, stop about ½ in.

USE A HANDSAW TO CUT THE KERF for wedging the tenon. Clamping the leg tightly on the sawhorse will hold it steady.

USE A HANDSAW TO MAKE WEDGES.
Make sure you've made all the vertical cuts to the baseline first. Then partially saw all the angled cuts before completing any one. Finish each cut in turn from right to left to liberate each wedge from the block.

CROSSCUT THE BLANK TO FREE the remaining wedges.

SPREAD GLUE ON EACH TENON and on the inside of each mortise and then push the leg in place. No pounding should be required. Then orient each wedge slot the way you want it before the glue sets.

short of where the curved shape of the leg begins. I oriented the saw kerfs parallel to the annual rings on each leg to achieve a consistent appearance.

2. For the wedges, the grain needs to go in the same direction as the grain in the tenon. To make them, first plane or cut wood 1 in. thick to match the diameter of the tenons. Then clamp the blank vertically on the sawhorse and clearly mark the shape and length of the wedges in pen.

3. Make the long straight cuts first, all the way to the baseline. Next, hold the blade at an angle and begin each angled cut. But don't cut all the way yet. Wait until each cut is well started before finishing a wedge. If you don't get each wedge started first,

it will be impossible to get the saw started for cutting the next one (**PHOTO B**). Finally, when you've made all the angle cuts for the wedges, crosscut the remainder (**PHOTO C**). Make several more than you need so you can choose and use the best.

4. Spread glue on each tenon and on the inside surfaces of each mortise. Then push the tenons into the mortises. Fit them hand tight (**PHOTO D**).

5. Before the glue has a chance to set, rotate the legs so that their wedge slots are aligned the way you want. Aligning the wedge slots parallel to the grain of the top can cause a split, so I orient the slots perpendicular to the grain.

E **DRIVE EACH WEDGE IN PLACE** after putting a bit of glue in each slot and on each side of the wedge. Make sure that the edges of each wedge align perfectly with the sides of its tenon.

F

A SMALL FLAT HANDSAW WORKS well to trim the tenons flush with the bench top. Use cardboard cut out around the tenon to keep the saw from gouging the surrounding surface.

6. Spread a bit of glue inside the wedge slots and then on each wedge. Drive them into place with a wooden mallet. Guide the wedges carefully so that their edges align with the edges of the tenons (**PHOTO E**).

7. After the glue is fully dried, use a handsaw to cut the tenons flush with the top. I use a piece of thin cardboard for backing to keep the saw from marring the surface. This will leave the tenons about ¹⁄₃₂ in. long. But a bit of spot sanding will make the tenons and wedges flush with the surface (**PHOTOS F**, **G**).

G

SAND THE TENONS FLUSH with a random-orbit sander. Work your way through the grits to obtain the best results.

Trim the legs

I CUT THAT LEG THREE TIMES and it still rocks: It's a typical problem, don't you think? Measuring and marking the legs to make the bench level is tough. Due to the irregularities of the slab, none of the legs can be the right length, so trimming is required.

1. Place the bench on a flat and level surface. Slide wedges under the legs until the bench is level and no longer rocks.

2. Measure the height at each end and each side to see if you need to level the bench in either direction.

On this bench, a shim about ¼ in. was required on one leg to make it stable. The opposite end was about ¾ in. taller, so I used a ¾-in. block to raise my pencil when marking how much should be cut off the legs on that end (**PHOTO A**).

3. Tilt the bench on its side and rest the legs on a mat or piece of carpet. Use a handsaw to cut the legs to length (**PHOTO B**).

4. Sand the edges smooth.

A

USE A BLOCK ABOUT ½ IN. THICK to support a pen (or pencil) to mark where you should cut the bottom of each leg.

HOLD EACH LEG IN TURN and trim with a handsaw at the cut line.

B

FINISHING WITH DANISH OIL

After you've spent so much time building your project, applying the finish can be fast and fun . . . or a disaster of drippy goo. I've found a simple method of finishing that avoids disasters and allows me to devote most of my attention to other parts of the creative process. It's Danish oil, and it works for me. My own favorite brands are Deft® Danish oil and Minwax® antique oil. Both give the same result: a clear finish that penetrates deeply into the wood, revealing its inner luster. Deft smells better, but Minwax is easier to find.

After sanding through to 320 grit, apply Danish oil liberally to all surfaces. Let that first coat sit for about a half hour and then apply a second coat. After another half hour or so, it will start to feel a bit sticky (but not quite hard) to wipe off when you wipe it with a cloth. Now is the time to wipe all surfaces clean with a dry cloth. A day later apply another coat, wait another half hour, more or less, until the oil just begins to offer resistance to the

APPLY DANISH OIL TO FINISH your bench.

cloth. Timing is everything. Rub the finish with a dry cloth, using it to spread and polish. You will get a finish that allows the real beauty of the wood to come out.

Finishing touches

THE BENCH IS ESSENTIALLY DONE except for a few details, including glides for the feet, a fix for a crack, and a few coats of finish.

1. I apply steel gliders to the ends of the legs to keep them from scratching the floor. They also visually separate the bench from the floor, which looks nicer **(PHOTO A)**.

2. To fix a small crack, I chose a very rustic fix: a nail. First cut the head off, then bend the nail into an oversized staple and sharpen both ends. Drill pilot holes on either side of the crack, then hammer the staple into place **(PHOTO B)**.

CENTER A GLIDE ON THE BOTTOM of each leg and tap it into place with a hammer or mallet.

HAMMER THE HANDMADE STAPLE ACROSS the crack, holding the stock from below to prevent further cracking.

Variation: Stump table

BEAUTIFUL PIECES OF WOOD don't just come as slabs. You may find a section of stump that can be used as part of a table, bench, or chair.

This project is from a maple tree that died in my town. After the tree was cut, the stump was cut flush with the ground. The piece was left on the roadside, where I found it on a walk. I saved it, knowing that it was beautiful and that someday it might be used for something.

Stump table

This table is made from a spalted maple stump, salvaged because it was too pretty to waste. As no two stumps are the same, no two tables could be the same. Design the frame to fit the dimensions of your stump, then support it within the frame on dowels.

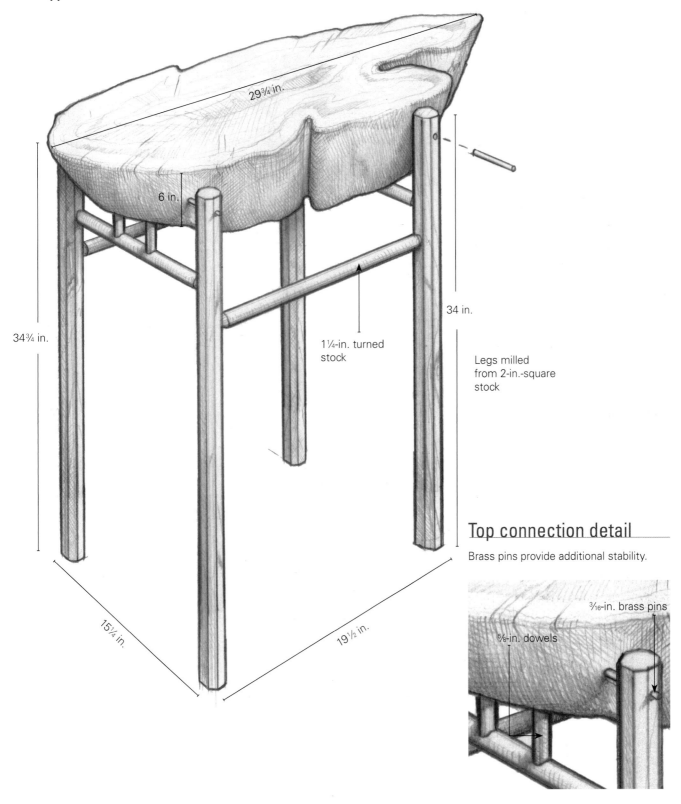

29¾ in.

6 in.

34¾ in.

34 in.

1¼-in. turned stock

Legs milled from 2-in.-square stock

15¼ in.

19½ in.

Top connection detail

Brass pins provide additional stability.

³⁄₁₆-in. brass pins

⅝-in. dowels

Sand the end-grain surface

Use an angle grinder, as shown in making the slab bench. Then use a random-orbit sander through a progression of grits to polish the top. Sanding end grain can take time. In this case, I am not interested in achieving a perfectly flat surface but simply revealing the beauty of the wood by removing the chainsaw marks.

SAND THE END-GRAIN surface of the stump.

Make and mortise the frame members

Make the frame members from 2-in.-thick stock, just as for the slab bench.

1. Bevel the edges of all the frame members, giving them an octagonal profile using the same process as on p. 48.

2. Lay out the mortises on the frame members.

3. To cut the mortises, use a drill press to make certain that the holes are square to the stock. When making the slab bench, freehand drilling was required. However, this table requires the accuracy and consistency only a drill press can provide so that the many mortises and tenons line up properly **(PHOTO A)**. I use a fence and stop block on the drill press to further increase accuracy.

4. Cut the stretchers to thickness and width but leave them an inch or so oversize in length so they can be held in the lathe.

A

USE A DRILL PRESS AND FENCE to position the mortises accurately.

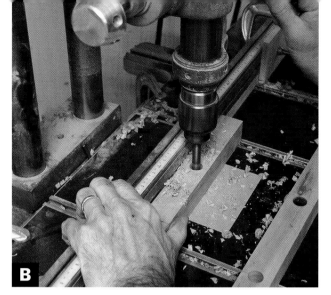

DRILL HOLES IN THE END STRETCHERS for dowels to be used to attach the stump to the frame.

5. Drill holes in the side stretchers for dowels to fit that can be used to support the stump **(PHOTO B)**. These parts shouldn't be octagons, as that isn't necessary and would interfere with alignment on the drill press.

Turn the stretchers and cut the tenons

I USE AN OPEN-END WRENCH TO CHECK the measurements as I turn to make sure I don't turn the tenons too small. An exact fit of the open-end wrench often results in a too-tight fit. But a little sanding will make it just right.

SAND THE STRETCHERS ON THE LATHE. Work your way through the normal grits, with the lathe running, of course.

You can use a lathe to turn the stretchers round and form the tenons at each end.

1. Mark and measure the position and length of the tenons carefully. I use an open-end ⅝-in. wrench as a diameter gauge **(PHOTO A)**. When the wrench slips in place, the tenon is sized to fit.

2. Sand the stretchers and tenons while still on the lathe **(PHOTO B)**.

3. Remove the stock from the lathe and trim the stretchers to length.

Assemble the frame

USE SLOW-SETTING POLYURETHANE GLUE for attaching the stretchers to the legs. First apply moisture to each joint, as it is the presence of moisture that activates the glue. I use a small dowel to move the glue around the mortise, coating all sides equally.

USE A FRAMING SQUARE TO CHECK that the tops of the legs are aligned after you clamp them together. Note the dry-fit dowels that help align the stretcher holes and the spacer block to keep the legs parallel.

Use slow-setting polyurethane glue to assemble the parts to allow time for adjustments during assembly. Urethane glue is activated by moisture in the wood.

1. Slightly wet the interior of the mortises and the surface of the tenons a few minutes before the glue is applied.

ASSEMBLE THE TABLE FRAME ON A flat surface. Note the clamps and spacers at the bottom holding the parts an equal distance from both ends.

2. Squeeze some glue in the mortises, and then use a small dowel to spread it evenly on the inside **(PHOTO A)**.

3. Clamp the parts together, sides or ends first. Check with a square that the legs are aligned at the top **(PHOTO B)**. I dry-fit dowels in the mortises to show me that I have the holes aligned properly for attaching the stump. I also place spacer blocks at the bottom, just to make sure the legs are parallel.

4. Allow time for the glue to set, then join the ends using the front and back stretchers. Again, spacer blocks and clamps as well as clamps at the joints are required to make certain the assembly is square. Assemble the frame on a flat surface so that it will rest steadily on the floor **(PHOTO C)**.

Attach the stump top

After the glue has set, turn the frame upside down over the stump. Map the locations for drilling mounting holes in the underside of the stump top, using the frame for reference. Measure the distance between the centers of the stretchers and transfer it onto the stump with a framing square (**PHOTO A**).

1. When you have determined the locations for the holes, drill them and dry-fit ⅝-in. dowels slightly longer than required for the final mounting of the stump (**PHOTO B**).

PLACE THE FRAME OVER THE STUMP to transfer the locations of the holes in the left and right stretchers so that the stump can be drilled for the dowels to fit.

DRILL THE DOWEL HOLES IN THE BOTTOM of the stump and dry-fit dowels in the holes. If they fit too tight, re-drill and wiggle the drill as it goes in and out to widen the holes.

2. Turn the stump over and use the technique described on pp. 52–53 for measuring and trimming the dowels to the right lengths to hold the stump in the frame **(PHOTO C)**. Because the underside of the stump is uneven, it is impossible to drill the dowel holes to a precise depth. Leveling the dowels on a flat surface is required, using the same technique used for leveling the legs for the slab bench.

3. Fit the top onto the frame, gluing the dowels and clamping as necessary.

USING THE SAME TECHNIQUE used for leveling the slab bench, mark the dowels and then trim them to length so they fit in the mortises to the same depth.

Plan B

TO TAKE WIGGLE OUT OF THE LIGHT FRAME, use brass rods drilled through the legs into the stump at each corner. Put tape on the drill bit to gauge the proper depth and use a doweling jig to align the hole accurately.

Every rustic project will engage you in problem solving, as nearly every piece is unique and it is impossible to anticipate everything that might come up. In making this stump table, I didn't anticipate how much wiggle the frame would have. A solution in hindsight would be to make the frame heavier in the first place, but I wanted a lighter look. So my solution? I fitted ³⁄₁₆-in. brass pins (brazing rod) from a welding supply shop through the legs into the stump at each corner. I used an extralong drill bit and a doweling jig to drill the pilot hole. The pins stopped the wobbling.

Variation: Slab chair

TO MAKE THIS CHAIR, follow the same steps used in making the slab bench, but use a grinder and coarse sanding disk to shape the seating spot. To form the laminated back, you will need to cut walnut into thin strips and glue them on a form.

Slab chair

This chair is made with a slab of spalted sycamore rescued from a tree left abandoned in a ditch. I carved the seat and laminated a back rail using thin walnut stock glued and clamped to shape in a simple mold.

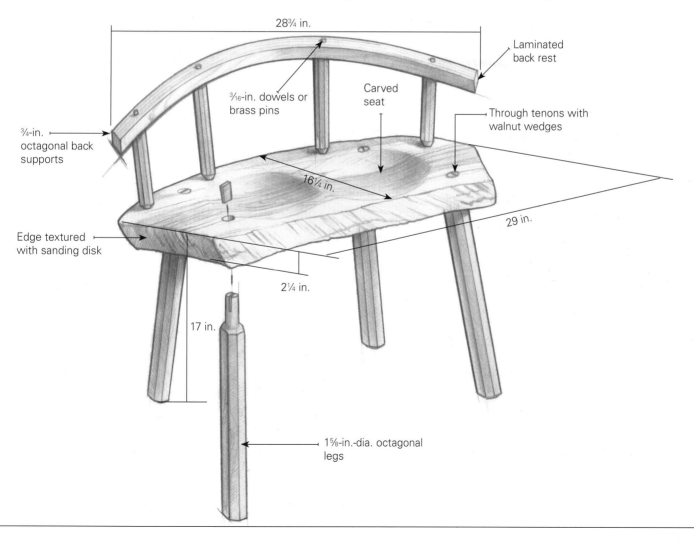

28¾ in.

Laminated back rest

³⁄₁₆-in. dowels or brass pins

Carved seat

Through tenons with walnut wedges

¾-in. octagonal back supports

16¼ in.

29 in.

Edge textured with sanding disk

2¼ in.

17 in.

1⅝-in.-dia. octagonal legs

MATERIALS FOR SLAB CHAIR

QUANTITY	PART	SIZE	MATERIALS	NOTES
1	Seat	2¼ in. by 16¼ in. by 29 in.	Spalted sycamore	
4	Legs	1⅝ in. by 1⅝ in. by 16½ in.	Black walnut	1-in. by 3-in. tenon on end. Rough length 18 in., then trim after fitting to seat.
4	Wedges	⅛ in. by 1 in. by 2½ in.	Black walnut	
13	Lamination strips for back	³⁄₆₄ in. by 1¼ in. by 42 in.	Black walnut	
2	Center spindles	¾ in. by ¾ in. by 8⅝ in. octagonal	Black walnut	⅝-in. by ⅝-in. tenons on each end
2	Outside spindles	¾ in. by ¾ in. by 7 in.	Black walnut	⅝-in. by ⅝-in. tenons on each end
4	Brass pins	⅞ in.		
4	Furniture glides	⅞ in.		Available from www.allglides.com, stock number SG87

Make the seat

I used a chainsaw to cut the slab of wood to shape, leaving saw marks and random edges. The shape of this seat came from removing parts that were unsound from decay.

1. Cut the seat to shape with a chainsaw, handsaw, or jigsaw. Then use an angle grinder and coarse sanding disk to carve out the seat recess. Sand the whole seat top smooth (**PHOTO A**).

2. Drill 1-in.-dia. mortises through the seat for the legs. Hold a scrap block under the drill's exit hole so you can avoid tearout.

A

USE AN ANGLE GRINDER TO SHAPE the seat hollows at the center of the slab.

SAND THE OCTAGONAL LEGS, facet by facet, up to 320 grit. Sanding them all at the same time helps keep the sander steady.

B

SAW THE LEGS TO LENGTH using a fine-toothed handsaw.

C

D

USE AN ANGLE GRINDER AND COARSE sanding disk to texture the edge of the seat. Tap the sanding disk lightly and randomly as you move the grinder along the edge.

3. Use the tablesaw to cut octagonal profiles on the legs. Then use the Veritas tenoner to cut 1-in.-dia. tenons on the ends.

4. Use a handsaw to cut a slot in the end of each tenon for fitting a wedge after assembly.

5. Sand the legs smooth before assembly **(PHOTO B)**.

6. Set the leg tenons in the seat mortises with glue. Drive wedges in from the top to secure the joints in the same way described to make the slab bench.

7. Use the technique shown on pp. 52–53 to measure the proper length for each leg and then saw them to length **(PHOTO C)**.

8. Texture the seat edge. I use an angle grinder and coarse sanding disk to make texturing strokes, tapping lightly against the edge of the seat **(PHOTO D)**.

Make the back

The back rail is made by cutting thin pieces of walnut stock and then laminating them to a curved form. The form is easy to make. I laid out the desired curve on a piece of plywood, then glued and screwed four large blocks of wood along the line.

1. Rip 1¼-in.-thick walnut into 13 uniform ³⁄₆₄-in.-thick strips.

2. Spread glue on the faces of the strips and clamp them to the form. Start at the middle and work your way to the ends of the stock. This will help avoid gaps between layers **(PHOTO A)**.

3. When the glue has dried, remove the back from the form and joint and plane the edges down to 1-in. thickness **(PHOTO B)**.

REMOVE THE LAMINATION FROM THE FORM and plane it down to 1-in. thickness after the glue has dried.

A

CLAMP THE WALNUT STRIPS TOGETHER EVENLY to the form. This takes a lot of clamps. Start at the middle and work your way to the ends. Apply extra clamps where there are gaps between the strips.

B

Attach the back

I use ¾-in.-thick octagonal spindles to hold the back rail to the chair. Use the same technique to make the spindles as for the legs. The tricky part is locating the correct position and angles for mortising in the back and the seat for the supports to connect the back rail to the seat.

1. Make the ¾-in.-dia. octagonal spindles on the tablesaw with the same techniques as for the legs.

2. Use blocks of scrapwood and clamps to hold the back in the desired position above the seat. Then mark the locations for the supports **(PHOTO A)**.

3. Use a long ³⁄₁₆-in.-dia. drill bit to drill down through the seat back and into the seat. This is the pilot hole for cutting mortises on the underside of the seat rail. It also marks the location for the mortises that you'll drill in the seat.

4. Drill ⅝-in. mortises in the underside of the seat back and then matching mortises in the seat.

5. Cut the spindles to length, then cut ¾-in.-long tenons on each end using a ⅝-in.-dia. tenon cutter.

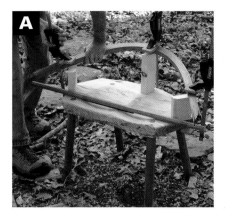

A

USE BLOCKS OF WOOD AND CLAMPS to hold the seat back to the seat so that you can mark the points for attaching it. The walnut stock resting on the seat is for the spindles.

B

CHECK THE LOCATIONS OF THE MARKINGS for the mortises in the seat before you drill.

C

USE A HAND-SAW TO CUT the seat back to length.

D

GLUE AND CLAMP THE SEAT BACK RAIL to the seat. First spread glue in the mortises and then use clamps to pull them tightly into place.

6. Glue the tenons into the mortises in the seat back and double-check the locations for the seat mortises before you drill **(PHOTO B)**. Drill the mortises.

7. With the spindles dry-fit in their mortises, saw the seat back ends to length. I marked the ends to the width and shape of the seat, then used a dozuki saw to make the cuts **(PHOTO C)**.

8. Fit all the spindles into the seat at the same time, with glue in each mortise. Use clamps to hold the tenons tight while the glue dries **(PHOTO D)**.

9. Fill the ³⁄₁₆-in. holes on the top face of the seat back with brass pins for a decorative accent.

10. Sand, then finish the chair with Danish oil.

Rustic Tree Branch Footstool

THIS STOOL provides a great way to put your feet up at the end of a long day. I based the size of this stool on one already in my home. By varying the lengths of the stretchers, you can easily make it any size you wish.

You can either use peeled branches or leave the bark on as shown in the variation.

Making a footstool first can help you master the skills required for more complicated projects like rustic chairs. You'll use the Veritas tenoner for forming the tenons. The stretchers and legs come together at approximately right angles rather than the complex angles used in making chairs. You can upholster your stool with seagrass twine or Shaker cloth tape.

This design uses dowels for the upper stretchers and branches for the lower ones. The dowels provide a better foundation for weaving the seat, giving more uniform results. The tree branch stretchers below add beauty and interest.

Rustic tree branch footstool

Rustic footstools—made with branches peeled of their bark or with bark intact, upholstered in Shaker tape or seagrass twine—will help to hone your skills for more complicated rustic work.

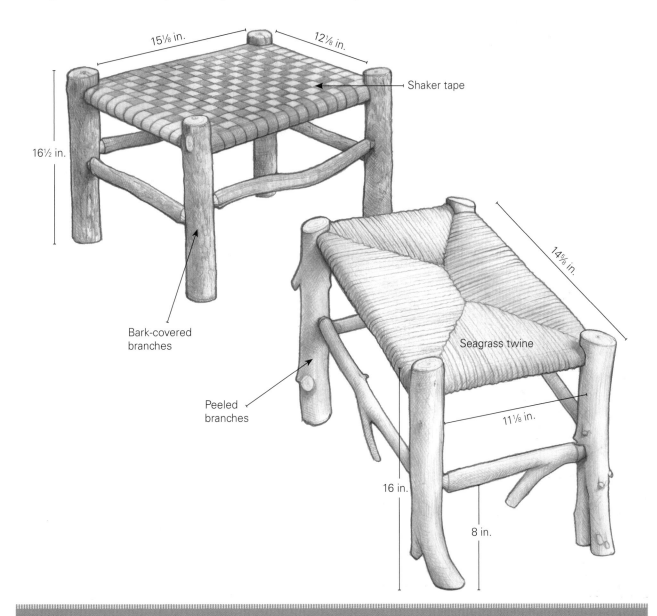

15⅛ in.

12⅛ in.

Shaker tape

16½ in.

Bark-covered branches

14⅝ in.

Seagrass twine

Peeled branches

11⅛ in.

16 in.

8 in.

BARK OR NO BARK?

You can make rustic furniture either with or without the bark. If you want bark on your finished work, harvest in winter while the leaves are off and the tree is dormant. In the spring and summer, the cambium layer will be swollen with sap and fragile. You'd best

plan to peel your branches. If you don't peel the bark off, it may loosen in time anyway. Peel it soon after cutting so that the bark is still wet and flexible.

Peeling the branches is more work but has some surprising advantages. Besides the lighter

color, the wood is smooth even without sanding. Also, powder-post beetles that sometimes infest rustic wood first enter through the bark. By removing the bark, you lessen the chances of infestation.

MATERIALS FOR RUSTIC TREE BRANCH FOOTSTOOL

QUANTITY	PART	ROUGH SIZE	FINISHED SIZE	MATERIAL	NOTES
STRIPPED BARK AND SEAGRASS STOOL					
4	Legs	2 in. dia. by 20 in.	2 in. dia. by 16 in.	Elm	Best to peel and dry 2 months before use
2	Lower front and back stretchers	1 in. to 1¼ in. dia. by 18 in.	1 in. to 1¼ in. dia. by 16⅞ in.	Elm	Put in lightbulb kiln to dry for 24 hours before use.
2	Side stretchers	1 in. to 1¼ in. dia. by 14 in.	1 in. to 1¼ in. dia. by 13⅜ in.	Elm	Put in lightbulb kiln to dry for 24 hours before use.
2	Upper front and back stretchers		⅞ in. dia. by 17⅜ in.	Hardwood dowel	
2	Seagrass twine	1-lb. rolls, 4.5 mm to 5 mm dia.			Available from www.seatweaving.org
4	Furniture glides	⅞ in.			Available from www.allglides.com, stock number SG87
NATURAL BARK AND SHAKER TAPE STOOL					
4	Legs	2 in. dia. by 20 in. long	2 in. dia. by 16½ in.	Hickory	
2	Lower front and back stretchers	1 in. to 1¼ in. dia. by 18 in.	1 in. to 1¼ in. dia. by 17⅜ in.	Hickory	Put in lightbulb kiln to dry for 24 hours before use.
2	Lower side stretchers	1 in. to 1¼ in. dia. by 14 in.	1 in. to 1¼ in. dia. by 14⅜ in.	Hickory	Put in lightbulb kiln to dry for 24 hours before use.
2	Upper front and back stretchers		⅞ in. by 17⅜ in.	Hardwood dowel	
2	Upper side stretchers		⅞ in. by 14⅜ in.	Hardwood dowel	
2	Shaker tape	1-in.-wide tape, 20 yd. each color			Available from www.seatweaving.org
4	Furniture glides	⅞ in.			Available from www.allglides.com, stock number SG87

Prepare the stock

I USUALLY HARVEST SMALL TREES, about 3 in. dia. at the base, or look for trees in a crowded forest that will benefit from thinning. From one tree, anything more than 1 in. dia. can be used.

1. For a stool without bark, harvest your material in the spring or summer and peel the bark off immediately.

2. I use a knife to dig under the bark and then pull, starting at the base and working my way up. You will find it gets easier as you go up toward the top, as the upper bark is thinner and more flexible. Use pliers to keep your hands from getting too tired. This would be hard work to do all day, but wood for a small stool can be stripped in very little time **(PHOTO A)**.

3. Allow the wood to dry for a month or longer if possible. This can help prevent major cracks from forming later (see the sidebar below).

4. Just before use, cut the parts for the bottom stretchers just longer than the required lengths and dry them in a drying box (see the sidebar on p. 71). This will reduce the moisture content so that the dry tenons will lock in place as the mortises in the legs shrink around them.

TO PEEL BARK OFF FRESH BRANCHES, start where you cut the branch off. Use a sharp knife to pry under the end of the bark. Then pull strips up toward the top.

PREPARING BRANCHES AND TWIGS

Although the best rustic work may look as though it just walked out of the woods, it is a mistake to think that you can just walk into the woods and make a chair. Natural wood is filled with moisture, each cell swollen like a fresh tomato. Each cell shrinks and hardens slightly as it dries, which means the whole stick shrinks over time. When you see splits and cracks in wood, it is this shrinkage from drying that is to blame.

In order for wood to dry, it has to be out of the rain in a place with some air circulation to carry away moisture. I have a shed where I hang sticks, limbs, and small trees to begin the drying process. I harvest materials for making furniture months in advance. Time to dry allows some of the shrinkage to take place before cutting joints.

Drill the mortises

THE LEG STOCK SHOULD BE AIR DRIED for a couple of months before use to help avoid cracks and checks from forming in the finished stool. It need not be completely dry, however, as the moisture in the stock will cause the legs to shrink, holding the stretchers tight.

B

USE AN AUGER BIT IN A POWER DRILL to cut the mortises for the stretchers. A dowel inserted in the first tenon hole aligns the stock and helps you cut the next at 90 degrees. A piece of black tape on the drill bit helps show when you've drilled to the desired depth of 1¼ in.

A

MARK THE MORTISE LOCATIONS on each leg using a story stick as a guide.

1. Cut your leg stock about 2 in. longer than the height of your finished stool. A handsaw will work well.

2. Make a story stick. On a piece of scrapwood the same length as the legs, record the positions of the various mortises required for making the stool. You should note that the locations for the stretchers are offset. This way the tenons for the front and sides don't intersect inside the leg.

3. Use the story stick to mark the locations of the mortises on each leg **(PHOTO A)**.

4. Drill ⅞-in.-dia. holes for the upper stretchers to fit.

5. Drill the mortises for the lower stretchers using a ⅝-in. drill bit to fit tenons cut with the Veritas ⅝-in. tenoner **(PHOTOS B, C)**. Place a dowel in an upper mortise to help you to gauge the angle as you drill. The dowel can be an actual stretcher or a short piece left over from cutting the upper stretchers to length.

C

KEEP THE DOWEL IN PLACE for aligning the drill while cutting the next holes, too.

WORK
SMART

An easy way to lay out the mortises for your legs is to use a story stick. First cut the stick the same length as your legs, then mark the locations of the mortises on the stick. Then transfer the markings from the stick to the legs before drilling. This will help make your measurements more consistent.

A DRYING BOX

A DRYING BOX CAN BE VERY SIMPLE: just a cardboard box with a trouble light at the bottom covered with a sheet-metal shroud. Stack the wood above the light and close the box.

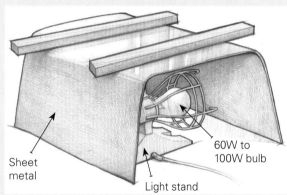

Sheet metal

Light stand

60W to 100W bulb

Wood shrinks as it dries. Old-time chair makers observed this and made use of it to make their chairs stronger and last longer. If a mortise is drilled in a piece of wood that is slightly damp and a tenon is cut on the end of a stick of dryer wood, the mortise will shrink and tighten around the tenon, making a stronger joint.

To make use of this principle, I dry the tenon stock in advance using a simple cardboard box with a lightbulb inside.

It is important to shield the hot bulb from the box and the wood to prevent a fire. I put the bulb in a sheet-metal housing that prevents it from touching the cardboard box. A common trouble light will work. A thermometer and humidity gauge inside help you check the progress of your wood. Cut a window in the top of the box and cover it in clear tape so you can observe the readings when the box is closed. Exact readings are not required, but you may be curious enough to observe the results.

Using the box is simple. Fill the box with sticks for your stretchers, turn on the lamp, and close the box. Keep them in the heated box for about 24 hours and their moisture content will be reduced enough.

Cut and fit the stretchers

A

WITH THE UPPER STRETCHERS FITTED in place, carefully measure the distance between the legs. Then add the depth of the mortises to determine the lengths of the lower stretchers.

I MAKE THE UPPER STRETCHERS FROM ready-made ⅞-in. dowel stock rather than uneven sticks. This provides a smoother and more uniform foundation for weaving the seat. The upper stretchers are completely hidden by the seating material, so more uniform stock won't detract from the rustic look but will make weaving easier, particularly for your first stool.

1. Cutting the upper stretchers to length is what determines the size of the stool. The exact length is not important, except that the sides should be the same length. In fact, you can hold them together and cut at the same time with a handsaw to be sure. When you have cut the upper stretchers, assemble the stool so you can measure for the exact length of the lower stretchers.

2. Measure the distance from leg to leg and add the depth of the tenons on both sides **(PHOTO A)**. I usually put one end of the tape in a mortise and

measure to the other side, then add the additional mortise depth to come up with a finished length.

3. Cut the stretchers to length.

4. Use the Veritas tenoner to cut tenons on each end of the stretchers. When working with small stock, you may be able to hold the workpiece in place by hand, depending on your physical strength. But for larger tenons on heavier stock you should use a clamp. The simple V-block on the sawhorse helps to level and hold the stretcher stock as you cut the tenons **(PHOTO B)**.

B

USE A VERITAS ⁵/₈-IN.-DIA. TENONER to shape the tenons on the ends of the stretchers after they are cut to length. On small stock that's only slightly larger than the diameter of the cutter, holding it by hand can be safe and secure. On thicker stock, clamping is best.

Assemble the frame

TRIAL-FIT THE STOOL BEFORE glue-up to make certain each piece fits as planned.

WORK SMART

When using polyurethane glue, be prepared with a cloth and mineral spirits to clean up any foam that forms on the joint. It is easiest to clean up while the foam is soft. The mineral spirits quickly dissolve excess before it hardens. If you wait too long, a chisel or sanding will be required.

SPREAD GLUE IN THE MORTISES using a smaller-diameter dowel to make sure every surface inside the mortise is coated with glue.

ASSEMBLY TAKES SOME CAREFUL PREPARATION and should not be hurried. Get your clamps and glue and have them ready. You will want to have a flat surface to work on.

1. Assemble the footstool first without glue for a trial fit to make certain it will go together as planned. Sometimes rotating the stretchers in place will help to find the way they fit best, and sometimes reversing them end for end can help. After all, the joints were cut without absolute precision **(PHOTO C)**.

2. When the fit is good, pull the stool apart and spread polyurethane glue in the mortises **(PHOTO D)**. Rather than disassembling and gluing up the entire stool at once, work in sections. I use a small-diameter dowel to spread the glue evenly on the inside surface of each mortise. Polyurethane glue can be messy and foam out of the joints, but it works well for rustic furniture because of the high moisture content in the wood. It also has a longer open time, allowing for some adjustment of parts during assembly.

3. Use band clamps to pull all the joints tight. Let the stool sit until the glue has set.

Trim the legs

MEASURE THE HEIGHT OF THE TOP stretchers to see that they are an even distance from the work surface. Shim under the legs to raise the height of a corner if needed. A straight stick placed across the stretchers makes it easier to measure.

TO TRIM THE LEGS TO AN EVEN, final height, you need a small block of wood and a pencil. If you're making a stool with the bark still on, you can't use a pencil to mark the legs for trimming. Use a saw instead for making your marks.

1. Check that the distance from the upper stretchers to the work surface is the same everywhere. This will help make sure the stool will stand level. If needed, place shims under the legs to obtain a uniform height at all corners (**PHOTO A**).

2. Use a block of wood as a height gauge for marking the ends of the legs (**PHOTO B**). Use a pencil or pen and draw all the way around the leg.

3. Saw the legs on the marks, using a handsaw. I prefer a Japanese pull saw because the fine teeth require less effort and it provides a very smooth cut (**PHOTO C**). The stool should sit squarely on the floor without rocking when done.

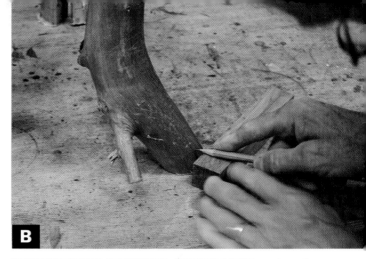

MEASURE THE BOTTOMS OF THE LEGS and mark them for trimming to make the stool level. I use a ¾-in.-thick block and a pencil.

TRIM THE BOTTOMS OF THE LEGS with a handsaw. Carefully follow the line you marked.

TRIM THE TOPS OF THE LEGS at a slight angle. Hold the stool in place with your free hand.

USE AN ORBITAL SANDER TO ROUND and smooth the ends of the legs and other sharp places. Steel wool or a Scotch-Brite® pad will smooth any rough spots along the legs or stretchers.

BRUSH DANISH OIL ON THE WHOLE FRAME. Make sure to coat any tight spots and the end grain of the legs. Wait 35 to 40 minutes and then use a dry cloth to wipe off any excess oil.

HAMMER THREE-PRONG FURNITURE GLIDES to the bottoms of the legs.

WORK SMART

When weaving a seat, use 3-yd. to 4-yd. lengths and join pieces when you get to the end. With seagrass or rush, tie or wire the ends together on the underside where the seam won't show. Longer pieces will get tangled and cause lost time and frustration.

4. Trim the tops of the legs to length. I cut these at a slight angle (7 or 8 degrees) to lower the profile at the corners **(PHOTO D)**.

5. Sand the ends of the legs and branch ends so they are smooth to the touch **(PHOTO E)**.

6. Coat the stool liberally with Danish oil, brushing it into any tight spots and paying particular attention to end grain **(PHOTO F)**. Wait 35 to 40 minutes and then use a dry cloth to wipe off any excess oil. Apply more coats as necessary.

7. After the finish dries, add three-prong furniture glides to the bottom of the legs. These serve three purposes. They prevent wear to the legs. They provide visual definition to the stool by lifting it from the surface on which it sits. And they provide just a bit of adjustment for leg length: If the stool rocks slightly, tap the glides on the two longer legs once with a hammer **(PHOTO G)**.

Weave the seagrass seat

WEAVING SEAGRASS TWINE TO FORM A SEAT is actually easy, particularly on a rectangular form like the frame of this stool. It is also easy to get mixed up and have to unweave work and start over. Fortunately, with practice it gets easier. You can fall into a comfortable rhythm and finish a seat like this in an hour or two, which will then last 50 years or more.

1. It is very awkward to work with long bits of seagrass twine, which can become tangled. So cut a piece about 3 yd. or 4 yd. long to start.

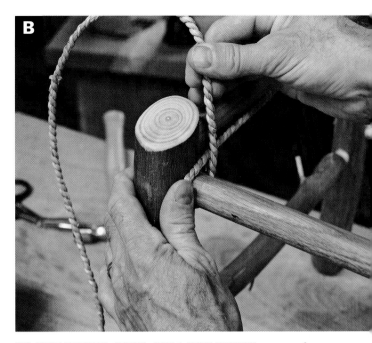

TO WEAVE THE SEAT, PULL THE TWINE over and around the front stretcher and then over and around the adjoining stretcher. Then pull the twine to the opposite corner and repeat the pattern, going over the stretcher, and then up and over its adjoining corner.

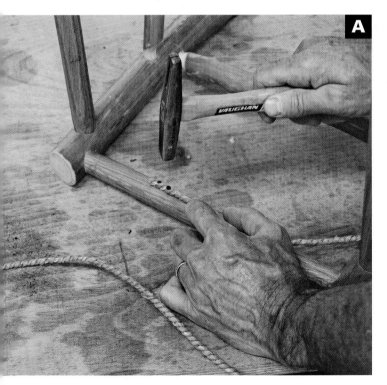

TACK THE END OF A 3-YD. OR 4-YD. LENGTH of seagrass twine to the inside of a side stretcher. This way the tacks will be hidden in the finished stool.

2. Begin the weave by tacking one end to the inside of a side rail where it won't show. Use two common carpet tacks for extra holding strength **(PHOTO A)**.

3. Here is where the pattern starts. Pull the twine up tight to the front stretcher and pass the twine over and around it. Then pull the twine up and over the side stretcher, capturing the run of twine along the side stretcher and pulling it tight to the side stretcher. If you remember always to go *over* the stretchers first, you can keep the pattern in the proper order **(PHOTO B)**.

4. Next, run the seagrass twine over the stretcher on the opposite side and over the intersecting stretcher at that corner. As you move from corner to corner, as long as you remember to keep going over each stretcher as you come to it, you will keep the pattern intact.

5. When you get to the end of the twine, attach it to a new piece. You can just tie a knot, but a bulky knot is harder to hide in the underside of the stool. Or you can unwind each end of the parts to be joined, push them together so the ends overlap by about an inch, then wrap them tightly with copper wire. Joining with this latter method makes a smaller yet more effective connection **(PHOTO C)**. By being careful to tie your joints where the twine will be underneath, they will be covered by subsequent wraps and invisible in the finished stool.

6. By following the same motions and pattern, corner to corner, and repeating over and over, the pattern gradually fills the space between the top stretchers. Try to use a uniform amount of pull as you work. Inconsistency can show up as loose spots in the finished stool. If you make a mistake but don't find it until later, don't be afraid to unwind and backtrack if needed. A few minutes saved now may be regretted for years to come **(PHOTO D)**.

7. When you fill the space on the two sides and still have some space to fill in the middle, go back and forth over the front and back stretchers in a figure-8 pattern until complete and either wire or tie the end in place.

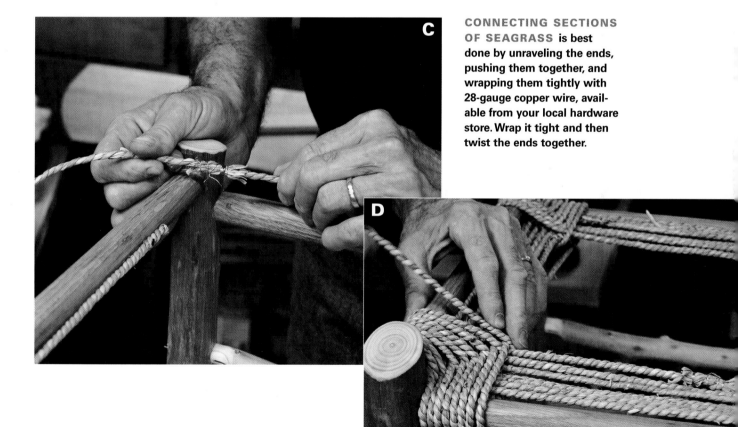

CONNECTING SECTIONS OF SEAGRASS is best done by unraveling the ends, pushing them together, and wrapping them tightly with 28-gauge copper wire, available from your local hardware store. Wrap it tight and then twist the ends together.

TRY TO BE CONSISTENT IN THE AMOUNT of tension you use in pulling the twine tight at each corner.

Rustic work can look easy, but when it comes to the materials it is easy to learn the hard way. There are unexpected things that can go wrong, so it's important to know about the materials before you go racing into the woods to gather wood for your first project.

One of the biggest disappointments is to discover bugs eating up your work. Powderpost beetles are the main culprit. They can live for years in a piece of wood, eating it, burrowing, and raising their young.

You can usually tell when powderpost beetles are active in wood. They push powder from small holes in the wood, where it becomes visible on carpets or bare floors. You can also detect their presence by checking the end grain on a cut piece. You will see small sawdust-filled tunnels in the layers just inside the bark.

If you notice powderpost beetle activity in wood you are using for a project, take aggressive action. The safest decision is to discard that wood and start fresh. However, there are three other strategies that can help.

First, the beetles are most often introduced to the wood through the bark. If you gather your materials in the spring and strip the bark, you are likely removing the possibility of infestation at the same time.

Second, heating wood in a kiln to 160°F will kill infestations. This is a technique used by some professionals.

The third option is to use Bora Care®, a mild insecticide that can be sprayed on the wood at the time of harvest as a preventative.

SMALL SAWDUST-FILLED TUNNELS FROM powderpost beetles are clearly visible in the layers just inside the bark.

LITTLE PILES OF DUST IN YOUR WOODPILE are a sign of powderpost beetle infestation.

Variation:
Weave a Shaker tape seat

I WOVE THIS SEAT ON A RUSTIC STOOL with the bark in place. But whether you are using peeled stock or stock with the bark in place, the directions will be the same. To use Shaker tape, you should design the length of the stretchers in even inches. This allows for a set number of 1-in.-wide wraps of tape. Using Shaker tape allows for the introduction of color to your work. You can weave the seat in a single color to match your home décor or mix colors for a more striking (or dynamic) effect.

1. Use carpet tacks to attach one end of the tape to the center of the front stretcher **(PHOTO A)**. Because the Shaker tape is 1 in. wide, plan your side stretchers (the distance between the legs) to be an even number of inches in length plus no more than about ⅛-in. extra width. This will keep the wraps of tape tight in relation to each other.

2. Next wrap the tape around the side stretchers until they're covered **(PHOTO B)**.

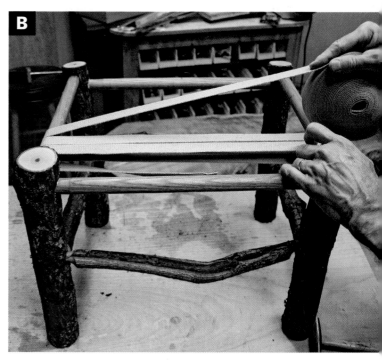

WRAP THE TAPE AROUND AND AROUND the side stretchers, maintaining a uniform tension as you go. For this first part, rather than cutting the tape in 3-yd. or 4-yd. lengths, I leave it in the roll to avoid having to join shorter pieces.

NAIL ONE END OF THE SHAKER TAPE to the inside of the front stretcher with two carpet tacks.

WHEN YOU GET TO THE END OF THE FIRST layer of tape, use a tack to secure it to the opposite stretcher. Cut off any excess tape.

ATTACH THE CONTRASTING COLOR TAPE to the front stretcher with two carpet tacks. Then wrap the tape over to cover the tack before beginning your weaving.

WEAVE THE CONTRASTING TAPE UNDER and over through the side-to-side tape, pulling with a uniform tension as you go.

3. When you get the correct number of wraps in place and tightly spaced, pull the end tight and tack it to the inside surface of the back stretcher **(PHOTO C)**. This part of the weaving is called the "warp."

4. Slide a layer of padding between the wraps of tape. You can use 1-in.-thick foam or fiber padding, cut to fit between the stretchers, less about ½-in. clearance in each dimension. Foam and fiber padding are available at sewing supply stores.

5. Using another color Shaker tape for contrast, tack one end to the inside of the front rail next to the left leg. Then wrap the tape over to hide the tack as you begin weaving through the warp. This part is called the "weft" or "woof" **(PHOTO D)**.

6. Weave the pattern under and over the warp, pulling with uniform tension and making certain that it goes straight across. If you aren't careful, the weft may begin to bow out in the middle as it passes from side to side. Take time to pull it straight as you go. I use 3-yd. or 4-yd. lengths of Shaker tape at a time. If you use longer pieces, it can get tangled and slow you down **(PHOTO E)**.

F

WORK SMART

When using Shaker tape to make a seat, plan the length of your stretchers to make the open space between the legs in even inch increments plus a small allowance, say ⅛ in. but no more. This will keep the tape woven tightly and prevent open spaces, giving a neater appearance to your work.

WEAVE THE UNDER-SIDE OF THE SEAT as well. On the underside you will see that the tape weaves at a slight angle as the tape forming the weft or woof compensates for square alignment on the top side.

G

WHEN YOU GET TO THE END of one piece, sew on another length. I use a sewing machine for speed, but hand stitching will work, too.

7. It is important to weave on both the top and bottom sides to get a tight weave, and it is good to show caring craftsmanship even where some may not notice. Weaving on the underside also helps to hold the top in more precise alignment **(PHOTO F)**.

8. When you get to the end of a piece of Shaker tape, add a new one by sewing them together. Plan the joint so it will be hidden by the warp underneath, and sew the two layers together to make the seam. You can sew by hand, but a machine is faster **(PHOTO G)**.

9. When you are finished, weave the remaining end of the tape back through on the underside and tension will hold it in place.

Slab-Top
Coffee Table

RUSTIC MATERIALS are frequently made even more interesting by contrasting design elements. This coffee table has a 22-in.-wide natural-edge spalted soft-maple plank top. The base is a trestle that uses an interesting joinery technique of overlapping parts log-cabin style. The natural-edge top contrasts with the more contemporary finely finished trestle base. You can easily modify this design to fit the size of slab you may have available.

But I also made a second base, which uses a branch-and-twig style construction more common in rustic work. In this case the more finely finished top contrasts with the rougher, bark-covered legs. Both versions build visual interest through the use of contrast. On both tables I used a rotary chisel to make the straight sawn surfaces more rustic in appearance. This task could have been done with a variety of other tools, like sanding blocks, gouges, rasps, or a grinder, adding to the visual and textural contrast within the piece.

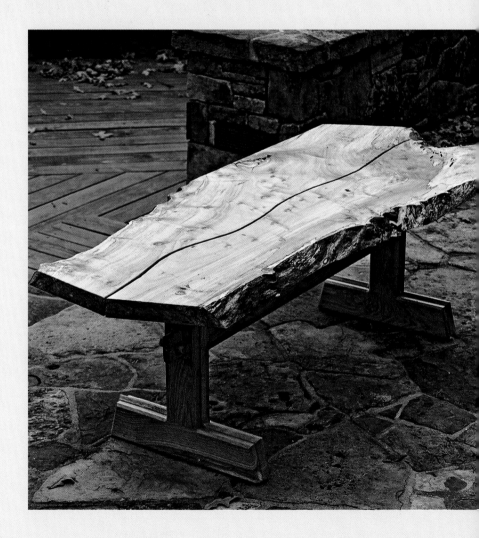

Slab-top coffee table

The slab-top table can be made with a contrasting contemporary trestle base or with natural tree limbs and branches using the Veritas tenoner to form the joints. Both tables are inspired by wide material harvested from a dead tree in my own community.

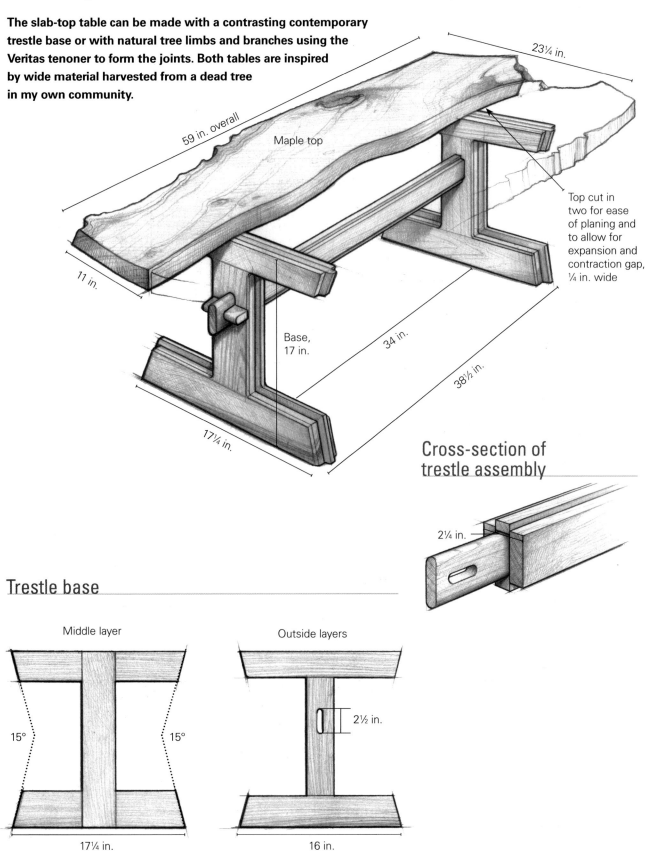

23¼ in.

59 in. overall

Maple top

Top cut in two for ease of planing and to allow for expansion and contraction gap, ¼ in. wide

11 in.

Base, 17 in.

34 in.

38½ in.

17¼ in.

Cross-section of trestle assembly

2¼ in.

Trestle base

Middle layer

15°   15°

17¼ in.

Outside layers

2½ in.

16 in.

MATERIALS FOR SLAB-TOP COFFEE TABLE

QUANTITY	PART	SIZE	MATERIAL	NOTES
1	Top	2 in. by 23 in. by 60 in.	Spalted maple	Cut at middle
TRESTLE BASE PARTS—CENTER				
2	Vertical parts	¾ in. by 4 in. by 17 in.	White oak	
4	Upper horizontals	¾ in. by 2⅝ in. by 6 in.	White oak	
4	Lower horizontals	¾ in. by 3⅝ in. by 7 in.	White oak	
TRESTLE BASE PARTS—OUTER				
4	Upper horizontals	¾ in. by 2¼ in. by 14¼ in.	White oak	
4	Lower horizontals	¾ in. by 3¼ in. by 16¼ in.	White oak	
4	Verticals	¾ in. by 3¼ in. by 11½ in.	White oak	
TRESTLE BOARD PARTS				
1	Center	¾ in. by 2½ in. by 40 in.	White oak	
2	Side strips	¾ in. by ½ in. by 34 in.	White oak	
2	Faces	¾ in. by 2¾ in. by 34 in.	White oak	
2	Wedges	¾ in. by 1 in. by 2¾ in.		
8	Screws	3-in. #6 hardened drywall		
4	Furniture glides	⅞ in.		Available from www.allglides.com, stock number SG87

Make the top

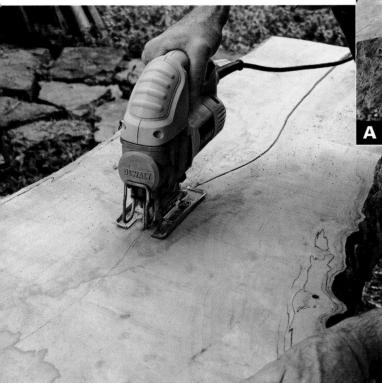

SKETCH A LINE IN PENCIL in the middle of the board, end-to-end. You can mirror features found in the grain or the overall shape of the board. But remember that a smooth line will be easier to follow with the saw than tight curves.

CUT ALONG YOUR MARKED LINE with a jigsaw and split the plank. Change the location of the sawhorses as needed to provide clearance on the underside of the cut.

WORK SMART

Interesting work starts with interesting materials. Keep your eyes open in your area and collect unusual sticks and boards. They will provide a foundation for building beautiful things.

THE FIRST CHALLENGE WAS TO SURFACE the 22-in.-wide board for the top with my 12½-in.-wide planer. This could have been done with hand planes and sanding, but if you have a planer and a jigsaw, there is an easier way that also adds interest to the finished table. I make a meandering end-to-end cut through the plank. Then I can run the two halves through the planer to flatten and make them the same thickness. Another advantage of this cut is that it allows better for the seasonal expansion and contraction of the top. The small gap in the middle narrows in wet weather and widens in the dry winter.

1. Begin by drawing a gently wandering line roughly through the center of the board. I prefer a meandering line to one that is straight, as this allows me to play off natural wood grain and figure in my design **(PHOTO A)**.

2. Use a jigsaw to cut along the line, dividing the board into two parts **(PHOTO B)**. I use a fine-toothed blade for a smoother cut. Alternatively, you could make this cut on a bandsaw.

SAW THE ENDS OF THE TWO PLANKS with angles similar to those on the crotch end. Use the features you find in your own planks to inspire your unique design.

C

FLATTEN THE TWO HALVES OF THE PLANK using a thickness planer. Plane one face of each board and then flip them end for end to plane the opposite faces. It may take several passes on each side to achieve a good surface if there are variations in thickness, especially around knots.

3. After the board is cut in two parts, it is easier to plane both parts down to uniform thickness. Plane the wood down in small increments for the best results **(PHOTO C)**.

4. To create a hint of symmetry I cut angles on one end that roughly reflect the angles of the crotch on the other end. On the crotch end, I left the marks of the saw that cut down the tree and the weathered surface, allowing these surfaces to tell a bit of the wood's story. These decisions are where a woodworker's natural creative judgment comes into play. Each piece of wood is unique, requiring unique decisions on the part of the craftsman **(PHOTO D)**.

5. I use a rotary chisel to create a texture on the edges of the stock. It is an easy way to hide the sawmarks. But it also provides an interesting contrast with the more finely finished top surface **(PHOTO E)**. I do this on both the cut between the two halves and the edges and ends of the boards.

E

USE A ROTARY CHISEL TO CREATE A TEXTURE on the sawn edges by tapping the surface gently. This will create a hand-chiseled look.

When making a table from a natural-edge plank, you will need to make the top first and then plan your base according to the dimensions of the finished top.

APPLY DANISH OIL LIBERALLY to darken and protect the wood.

The texture eases the transition between the sawn and natural edges.

6. Sand all the surfaces of the tabletop. Using a random-orbit sander I move through a progression of grits, from 100 grit through 320 grit.

7. I use Danish oil finish that penetrates into the wood, building up a slight gloss over successive coats. One additional advantage of this approach is that I can give it extra protection with a spray coat of satin polyurethane after the Danish oil is dry, usually 24 hours. I use the polyurethane when I know the table will be subjected to hard use and requires extra protection or when the gloss from the Danish oil is uneven **(PHOTO F)**.

TEXTURES WITH A ROTARY CHISEL

The rotary chisel made by Creative Technologies (www.rotarychisel.com) bears a strong resemblance to a router bit, but it should not be mistaken for one. When mounted in a die grinder or a RotoZip®, the rotary chisel can create a rustic, hand-carved texture.

Before using it on a project you plan to keep, practice on scrapwood to make sure you understand the technique and how to achieve the pattern you like. I use it by lightly tapping the spinning tool on wood. You will find that the direction of wood grain will have some influence on the results. Work from uphill toward downhill as you follow wood grain.

Working against the grain will not give the same level of crisp result. Be careful not to hold too long in one place.

Clamp the piece of wood you are texturing tightly to a sawhorse or workbench so you can have both hands safely on the tool. Holding the work in one hand and the tool in the other is an invitation to injury. Wear safety glasses.

Although the rotary chisel is available in a variety of shapes, my favorites are the U-shaped cutters that leave marks like a gouge, giving the impression of hours of hand carving.

Make the trestle table base

THE DESIGN OF THIS BASE COMES from the simple concept of the log-cabin corner. By overlapping parts a rigid structure can be created. Although a similar base could be made using solid, thick materials and mortise-and-tenon joints, this technique makes very strong long-lasting construction easier using fewer tools. I first saw it used for furniture in *Fast Furniture* by Armand Sussman. Although I made my base using white oak planed on both sides to uniform dimensions, an even more rustic base can be made by just planing the center boards on two sides and planing the outer boards only on the inside surfaces, leaving rough weathered wood to present a rustic look.

1. I begin by ripping planed stock on the tablesaw to the dimensions shown in the materials list (**PHOTO A**). Here I used white oak, but any other wood will work as well. This same work can be done with a hand-held circular saw and ripping guide.

2. I use a crosscut sled on the tablesaw to cut the parts accurately to length (**PHOTO B**).

3. Join the parts of the center layer with biscuit joints. This process could be done without this step and the next, but I get more precise results this way. Building up this center layer with biscuits and glue holding the parts together first will make it easier to align the parts that are attached to the outside (**PHOTO C**).

A

RIP STOCK INTO PIECES FOR THE TRESTLE BASES according to the dimensions in the materials list.

B

USE A SLED AND STOP BLOCK ON THE TABLESAW to cut the parts to length. First trim one end square, then slide the stock against the stop block and cut. Each piece cut in this manner will be exactly the same length.

C

CUT #20 BISCUIT SLOTS IN THE middle-layer pieces to join the parts.

4. Glue and clamp each middle layer together, giving special attention that all the edges line up. The extra C-clamps shown in the photo are intended to ensure alignment (**PHOTO D**).

5. Use the tablesaw to trim the angled ends on the assembled trestle core sections. Set the miter gauge at 15 degrees. Place the workpiece against the gauge. Then turn the saw on and make the cut. Turn the saw off between cuts. Flip the piece over to make each successive cut (**PHOTO E**).

GLUE AND CLAMP THE PARTS TOGETHER to make the middle sections. The C-clamps make sure the parts align flat.

USE THE TABLESAW TO TRIM THE ENDS of the base units to a 15-degree angle. Mark the position of the cut on the stock, place the assembly on the tablesaw, and get it in position while the saw is turned off. Then turn the saw on and make the cut. Turn the saw off before removing. This cut can also be made with a hand-held circular saw or a jigsaw.

LOG-CABIN JOINERY

One of the easiest ways to secure pieces of wood in a lasting structure is with a kind of log-cabin joint. In this simple joint, pieces of wood are overlapped, glued, and nailed to each other, forming a simple-to-make joint with great strength. This joint has innumerable uses. The idea comes from log cabins, in which layer after layer of logs are stacked with corners overlapping. Houses built this way can last hundreds of years.

The base of this table uses the same principle but uses only three layers. I biscuit the center structure together, then add strength with layers on each side.

You can add interest by offsetting the layers slightly (as in this project). Or the layers can be a perfect match, with all the edges aligned. Another option is to plane the materials uniform for the center layer and then use roughsawn and random-thickness wood on the outer layers, making your project more rustic than the base shown here.

CUT THE REST OF THE PARTS for the base assemblies. Again, use the miter gauge on the saw, set at a 15-degree angle.

CHAMFER THE EDGES OF THE CENTER assemblies of the base units with a router. You need to do this before the sides are glued in place.

SPREAD GLUE ON EACH PART BEFORE nailing it to the middle-layer assembly. Note that I avoid applying glue too close to the edge, where it will squeeze out and make a mess to be cleaned up later.

6. I chamfer the edges of the center trestle sections with a router. However, you can choose your own profile. A roundover would work as well and be just a bit easier when it comes time to do the sanding (**PHOTO F**).

7. Cut the outside layer parts to length. Then cut the 15-degree angles at the ends of the horizontal parts (**PHOTO G**).

8. Apply glue liberally on the insides of the parts, but avoid the edges, where squeeze-out can cause a mess (**PHOTO H**). It is challenging to learn just the right amount of glue required, and experience is the key. If you get excessive squeeze-out, wipe it up very thoroughly with a damp cloth. Some detailed cleanup can be done with a sharp chisel when the glue turns leather-hard but before it is fully cured.

USE A PNEUMATIC NAIL GUN TO ATTACH the side pieces to the middle layer. Hold it carefully in position while nailing.

I

WORK SMART

Clean the dust bag on your random-orbit sander each time you change species of wood. Then save the sawdust that you collect. By mixing it with Duco cement you can make fast-drying wood filler that will match that species exactly.

USE HOMEMADE FILLER TO FILL the nail holes. I use Duco cement and some sanding dust from the same species of wood to make the filler.

J

9. Use a pneumatic nail gun to attach the parts together **(PHOTO I)**. When nailing, avoid the area where you will need to drill the mortise later for attaching the two trestles with the center support. You can assemble the trestles without nailing, just glue and clamps alone. But it is difficult to hold the parts in position without the nails. And you would have to clamp each part one at a time.

10. The nail holes can be easily filled and become nearly invisible in the finished table. I make my own filler by collecting sanding dust from the random-orbit sander. Collect wood dust of the same species and mix it with clear Duco® cement into a thick paste. You will want to work with a small dab at a time, as the glue dries very quickly **(PHOTO J)**.

Mortise the trestle legs

THIS IS ACTUALLY THE HARDEST PART of making this table. You need to mark out the position of the mortises accurately, then drill from both sides. This is important to avoid tearout on the underside when the drill exits the wood. Next, some chisel work is required. So, if you are an inexperienced woodworker, please welcome the opportunity to learn a new technique.

1. Mark the beginning and end, or length, of the mortise on the trestle with a pencil.

2. Set a marking gauge so that the pin scribes at the center of the assembly whether you scribe from one side or the other. Then pull it toward you between your pencil marks to scribe the centerline for drilling **(PHOTO A)**.

USE A POWER DRILL AND AUGER BIT to make a series of holes, forming the mortise. Drill the outside holes first, then drill out the spaces between, each time centering the drill on the marking-gauge line.

USE A WIDE CHISEL TO FINISH FORMING the walls of the mortise in the trestle base. Chop from both sides in toward the middle to avoid tearout of wood on the opposite side.

3. Use a power drill, brace and bit, or drill press to drill pilot holes for forming the mortise. If using an auger bit, the drill can exert a great deal of force, so clamp the workpiece down to a solid surface to hold it steady. Also drill in from both sides to avoid tearout where the drill exits the wood **(PHOTO B)**. Space the holes to overlap, so that most of the waste wood is removed by the drill.

4. Next use a wide chisel to remove the remaining stock between the holes, finishing the mortises. Chisel in from one side and then turn the workpiece over to finish the cutting from the other side **(PHOTO C)**.

USE A MARKING GAUGE TO LOCATE the center of the assembly and mark for drilling the mortises for the trestle board.

Make the trestle

B

GLUE AND CLAMP THE SIDE STRIPS TIGHTLY to the trestle board first, aligning the ends with your scribe mark. The ends of the strips form the inside shoulder of the trestle board, so align them accurately.

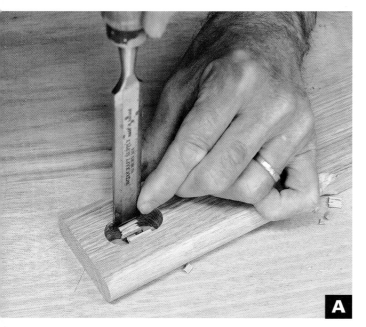

A

PARE OUT THE WOOD REMAINING between the mortise holes on the trestle board. Pare from both sides to avoid tearout.

C

GLUE AND CLAMP THE FACE PIECES to the trestle center, being careful that they align accurately.

THE TRESTLE, LIKE THE LEGS, HAS THREE LAYERS glued and nailed together. The longer center forms the tenon for attaching it to the legs, and the side strips and faces attached to each side provide a firm shoulder that butts up against the legs to hold it in position.

1. Plane stock for the center board in the trestle assembly to ¾ in. thick. It should fit into the mortise perfectly. If not, it can be planed down slightly to fit, or the mortise can be widened with a chisel.

2. Use a ⅜-in. quarter-round bit to round the corners about 4 in. or 5 in. in from the ends. You only need to round the center of the trestle partway, just

beyond the point where it's hidden inside the side strips and faces.

3. Drill the mortises in the trestle center. These will capture the wedges when assembling the table. Finish the mortises by paring the waste out with a chisel (**PHOTO A**). By paring from both sides, you can avoid tearout.

4. First glue and clamp the side strips on the edges of the trestle board (**PHOTO B**). After those strips have been glued in place, add the face pieces to the trestle (**PHOTO C**). You can use a nail gun in place of clamps to hold these parts in place as the glue sets.

Make wedges

MAKING WEDGES IS EASIEST and safest to do by hand.

1. Rout the corners of a piece of wood ¾ in. thick (or the width of the mortise in the trestle board), 3 in. wide, and about 8 in. to 10 in. long. Use a ⅜-in. quarter-round bit.

2. Mark a line at a slight angle (2 or 3 degrees) along the length of the board to form the shape of the wedge.

3. Saw out the wedge with a fine-tooth handsaw **(PHOTO A)**.

4. Slide the wedge tightly in place and mark it for trimming to length. I cut each end at a slight angle so that it aligns on both sides of the trestle **(PHOTO B)**.

SET THE OVERSIZE WEDGE WITH A HAMMER, then mark to trim it flush with the edges of the trestle base.

MARK AND SAW THE END of a board for the wedges.

Attach the base to the top

ATTACHING THE BASE TO THE TWO TOP boards is easily done with wood screws. I used four screws to attach each board. These connect through the upper part of the base and are just a few inches apart. This reduces the impact of expansion and contraction of the top boards, as they can freely expand both toward the center gap and toward the outside.

1. Drill and countersink pilot holes through the trestle legs. I position the screws about 3 in. apart and angle them in from opposite sides of the upper portion of the base.

2. Wax the 3-in. screws before driving them in place. This makes the screws go in easier and lessens the likelihood of breaking or stripping at the head. I use beeswax as a lubricant.

3. Drive the screws in. You need to be very careful in the selection of screw length so that they don't pass all the way through the tabletop. If your top is thinner or the base a different dimension, be sure to recalculate the proper screw length. Leave a ¼-in. space between the top halves when you screw the base to them.

SECURE THE BASE TO THE TWO top halves with 3-in.-long screws. Two screws into each half from each base section will keep the top secure.

Variation: Tree branch base

TO MAKE A TABLE BASE WITH TREE LIMBS is a very simple process thanks to the Veritas tenoner. I used winter-harvested hickory and dried the wood for three months before use. Nearly any hardwood could be used. For an added variation, consider stripping the bark as shown in "Rustic Tree Branch Footstool" on p. 66.

Twig base variation

Overall height 19 in.

Cross stretchers stiffen table

Mortise-and-tenon joints

Sticks, with or without bark

Legs, 17 in.

17½ in.

Base, 37 in.

15 in.

Base width should be adjusted to allow for differences in top width.

Cut the joinery

1. Dry only the top ends of the legs for about 24 hours in a drying box (see p. 71). To fit just the ends in the box, poke holes through the sides and rest the legs on another box. This way the ends will be drier where they will be tenoned, whereas the lower portion will remain slightly damp where they will be mortised (**PHOTO A**). You can dry the stretcher stock at the same time.

2. Measure for and drill mortises in the legs using a ⅝-in. bit. Clamp the legs tightly in place for this operation and be careful that your drill is held vertical for both holes (**PHOTO B**).

A

B

USE A DRYING BOX TO DRY the stretchers and the ends of the legs. Poke holes in the side to accommodate the ends, but not the rest of the legs, in the box.

USE AN AUGER BIT IN A HAND-HELD drill to cut the mortises in the legs. Clamp the legs firmly and keep the drill as vertical as you can.

C

CHECKING WITH A LEVEL, clamp the stretchers as level as you can to the sawhorses. With irregular stock, this will be difficult, but do your best.

MAKE USE OF THE BUILT-IN LEVEL on the Veritas tenoner as you adjust your position for forming tenons.

D

3. Cut the ⅝-in. tenons on the stretchers. It helps to level the stock first and then use the bubble level on the tenoner to check the way you hold the drill. If the stick is level and you make an effort to keep the drill level, you are more likely to get good results **(PHOTOS C, D)**. I use a 2x4 with V-cuts clamped to a sawhorse to steady the round sticks. The V-cuts keep the stock from rolling and can be adjusted in height to make leveling the stock easier.

WORK
SMART

Insert a piece of dowel in the body of the Vertias tenon cutter to act as a depth stop. You'll cut every tenon just the right length.

Assemble the base

1. Spread polyurethane glue in the mortises and then fit the tenons in place. You will find that they may fit best rotated one way or another **(PHOTO A)**.

2. Lay the parts down on a level surface to prevent twist as the glue dries. This may be hard to do with more wildly shaped stock **(PHOTO B)**.

3. If the legs are too large or misshapen for the tenoner to work effectively, you can remedy the problem with a saw or drawknife. The idea is to whittle the end down until the tenoner is able to cut well **(PHOTO C)**.

USE A SMALLER-DIAMETER DOWEL to spread the polyurethane glue to all the inside surfaces of the mortises.

USE CLAMPS TO PULL THE LEGS TIGHT on the stretchers as the glue sets. Avoid marring the bark by using soft pads or plywood blocks on the clamp faces.

USE A DRAW KNIFE TO REDUCE the size or remove a knot or twig from the leg ends if the tenoner cannot start the cut on its own.

E

GLUE AND CLAMP CROSSPIECES
at the tops of the assembled leg sections.

USE A 1-IN. VERITAS TENONER to form tenons
on the ends of the leg assemblies. These must be
clamped firmly in place while you work.

4. Cut the tenons on the top ends of the legs.
Make sure the leg sections are well secured. The
larger 1-in.-dia. tenoner takes a big bite and the
½-in. drill I use has a lot of torque **(PHOTO D)**.
Keep both hands on the drill while working.

5. Drill mortises in the cross stretchers and fit
them on the tenons at the tops of the leg assemblies
with polyurethane glue. Clamp them tightly and let
them set **(PHOTO E)**.

6. Use a handplane to make a level flat on the tops
of the cross stretchers. This prepares them for joining to the tabletop **(PHOTO F)**.

7. Use screws to attach the leg assemblies to the
tabletop. I drill and countersink the holes first

PLANE THE TOPS OF THE LEG ASSEMBLIES to
provide a flat surface for attaching the top boards.

DRIVE SCREWS THROUGH THE CROSS STRETCHER to secure the leg assemblies to the top. Drilling pilot holes for the screws is essential.

WITH A DIAGONAL STRETCHER CLAMPED in place, use it as a guide to drill the mortise at the proper angle.

to avoid splitting the stretchers. Again, be careful about the length of the screws so that there is no danger of them breaking through the tabletop **(PHOTO G)**.

8. Next I add diagonal stretchers between the legs to stiffen the base. Without these to give strength, the table would wiggle, so they are important. Drill mortises in the stretchers one at a time **(PHOTO H)**. After fitting one tenon, put the diagonal stretcher in place to locate the place and proper angle for the matching mortise. Then cut the stretchers to length and cut the tenons. You will have to pry the legs apart slightly to get the tenons to fit in their mortises. Pull or clamp across the diagonals to pull them tight before the glue sets.

9. After the table is complete, put it on a stable flat surface. Shim the legs as needed to level the table at both ends and side to side. Then trim each leg as necessary to both level the table and make it the right height **(PHOTO I)**.

TRIM THE LEG ENDS with the table leveled. Clamp guide blocks to the legs as a saw guide and trim all the legs the same distance from the bench top.

Rustic Chair

MAKING A RUSTIC chair looks like it might be easy, and it can be. The hard part is to make one that is comfortable as well as strong and beautiful. Just like any woodworking design project, practice can lead, in time, to improvement and perfection.

In this chapter I'll give you the techniques to make your first chair. It will hopefully launch your exploration of chair design, leading to your refinement of technique and the development of your skills.

This chapter includes two chairs: a straight chair made with a solid wood seat and an armchair made with a seagrass twine seat. Both of these projects build on the skills you developed in "Slab-Top Coffee Table" on p. 82.

Rustic chair with hickory branches and carved walnut seat

This chair features hickory branches with the bark still on and a carved walnut seat and back.
The frame of this chair is made to fit the hand-carved seat. However, no two pieces of rustic wood are alike.

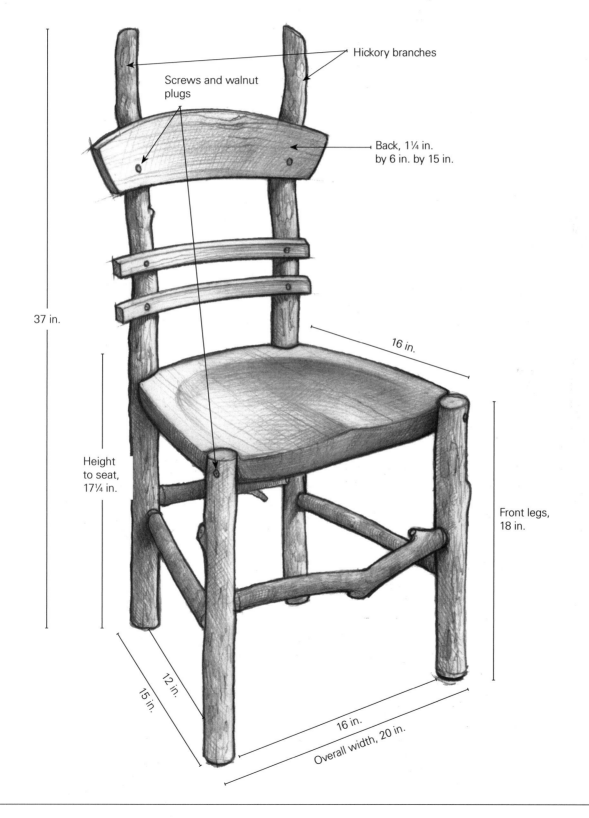

Hickory branches

Screws and walnut plugs

Back, 1¼ in. by 6 in. by 15 in.

16 in.

37 in.

Height to seat, 17¼ in.

Front legs, 18 in.

12 in.

15 in.

16 in.

Overall width, 20 in.

MATERIALS FOR RUSTIC CHAIR

QUANTITY	PART	ROUGH SIZE	FINISHED SIZE	MATERIAL	NOTES
1	Seat		1½ in. thick by 16 in. by 17 in.	Black walnut	
2	Back legs	1½ in. dia. by 39 in.	1½ in. dia. by 36½ in.	Hickory or other available wood	
2	Front legs	1¾ in. dia. by 21 in.	1¾ in. dia. by 18 in.	Hickory or other available wood	
1	Front stretcher		1 in. dia. by 18 in.	Hickory or other available wood	
1	Back stretcher		1 in. dia. by 13¾ in.	Hickory or other available wood	
2	Side stretchers		1 in. dia. by 13¾ in.	Hickory or other available wood	
1	Upper seat back		1¼ in. by 3⅝ in. by 14 in.	Black walnut	Cut from shaped stock 1¼ in. by 6 in. by 14 in.
2	Lower seat back		1¼ in. by 1 in. by 13¼ in.	Black walnut	Cut from shaped stock 1¼ in. by 6 in. by 14 in.
4	Screws		3-in. #8 flathead		
6	Screws		1⅝-in. #6 drywall		
10	Plugs		⅜ in. dia. by ⅜ in.	Black walnut	Available from www.rockler.com
4	Furniture glides	⅞ in.			Available from www.allglides.com, stock number SG87

Start with the seat

FOR MOST CHAIR MAKING, THE SEAT is the last step. But the seat comes first when making a chair with a carved solid wood seat. Working from its dimensions is critical to the design of the rest of the chair. You can begin with a wide plank of solid wood, or you can glue up boards to get the needed width.

1. Make a half-seat template of the finished chair seat. This ensures the seat will be symmetrical. Use a jigsaw to cut the template out of thin Masonite® or MDF. Sand the edges a little, then trace the shape on the seat blank **(PHOTO A)**. Mark all sides of the template, then flip it over to mark the other side. This is much easier than trying to make a symmetrical pattern for a whole seat and uses half the materials. Save the template for the next chair.

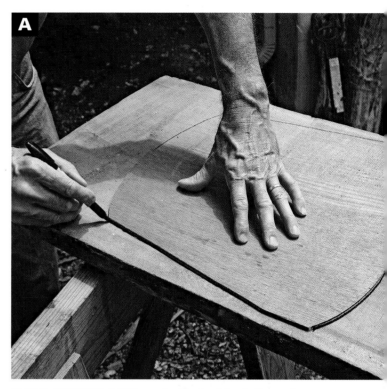

MARK OUT THE SEAT on the blank with a half-template.

DESIGNING A CHAIR

Chairs are widely regarded as among the most difficult woodworking projects. They need to be strong enough to support the body, yet light enough to be easily moved around. In addition, they need to fit the body and its proportions with a reasonable degree of comfort. So there are a variety of considerations in the design of a simple chair.

There is no better way of designing chairs than by embarking on a personal study using your own body and a tape measure. Sit in a variety of chairs to see how they feel, and then use your tape measure and make notes. How high is the seat? Is it the same height in the front as in the back? What is the length of the seat? How high is the back? How much does it lean back? How wide is the seat? If it has arms, how long are they and at what height?

If I were telling you how to make a chair in a standard design, you could avoid all this personal research. But there can be no standard designs in making a rustic chair, as the variations in the available materials determine the design to a large extent. As a chair maker you will also have to become a student of design. Rustic chairs can be made in any style you might imagine. Your examination of existing chairs will help guide you to success.

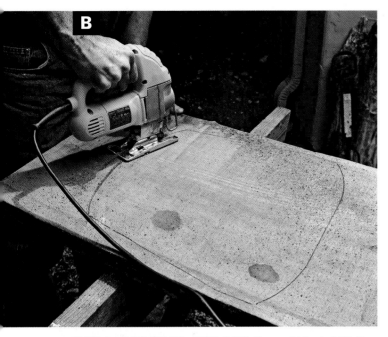

USE A JIGSAW TO CUT OUT the seat blank. I tilt the blade about 15 degrees inward to reduce the amount of shaping that will need to be done on the underside.

USE AN ANGLE GRINDER with a coarse, 60-grit sanding disk to rough out the shape of the seat.

2. Use a jigsaw to cut out the seat. I tilt the blade about 15 degrees inward. This reduces the amount of shaping required on the underside of the seat **(PHOTO B)**.

3. Shape the seat to conform to the body with an angle grinder and coarse sanding disc. I start with 60 grit and work my way to finer grits. It helps to outline the areas to be sanded. You may find that your fingers and hands are more sensitive than your eyes in assessing the shape and determining which parts still need attention from the coarse disk **(PHOTO C)**. Move from coarse to fine grits as you work, and change to a random-orbit sander when you reach 120 grit **(PHOTO D)**.

4. Use the angle grinder to shape the bottom corners of the underside of the seat **(PHOTO E)**. Finish with a random-orbit sander.

USE A RANDOM-ORBIT SANDER to finish sanding the shaped seat. Start with 120 grit and work your way to finer grits.

GRIND THE UNDER-SIDE OF THE SEAT with the coarse disk, rounding the edges (but leaving a crisp edge along the top). Change to a 100-grit sanding disk as you get close to completion.

E

ANGLE-GRINDER TECHNIQUE

Using an angle grinder to shape wood will take practice. First make sure the wood is held tightly with clamps. Then, move your arms in a circular motion, never holding the grinder long in one place. Turn the tool off frequently and check the surface by moving your hand across it. You will find that your hands are more sensitive than your eyes at finding irregularities. When you find high spots, narrow your motions to grind in that spot. You can bear down hard with the tool when you want to go deep, but a light motion, never lingering long in one spot, will give the best results. If this is your first time with this tool, practice on scrapwood first.

Make the chair frame

YOU CAN MAKE CHAIRS FROM WILDLY misshapen and mismatched stock. But for your first, you will want to keep things a bit simple.

1. Select materials that are somewhat uniform in size and shape. The back legs should be selected first, as they are critical to the successful design of your chair **(PHOTO A)**.

SELECT THE BACK LEGS CAREFULLY, laying them out so they can be compared to each other. Symmetrical back legs, with a similar curvature, will make the chair much easier to build.

A

Success in making a rustic chair often starts when the craftsman first steps into the woods. Most rustic chair makers look at many saplings before harvesting the first one, and as you gain experience, you will develop an eye for which small trees will best serve in chair making.

After the wood is cut and partially dried, carefully select stock for your back legs first. These are the hardest parts to find, and you will find it easiest to make a chair if you select back legs that are somewhat uniform in size and general curvature.

2. Cut the front and back legs to length. I make my parts longer than required in the finished chair, as I always cut off at least 1 in. from the top and 1 in. from the bottom at the end.

3. Use a story stick to lay out the positions of the various mortises (as in "Rustic Tree Branch Footstool" on p. 66). You can mark the positions directly by measuring, but you will find the story stick useful if you want to make a similar chair later on.

4. Select the cross-stretcher stock for the front and back assemblies and cut them to length. The length of the stretchers should be derived from the width of your seat. Measure the width of the seat and cut your stretchers long enough so that the tops of the legs will nest in recesses sawn at the corners of the seat.

USE BAND CLAMPS TO HOLD THE front and back leg assemblies while the glue sets. The band clamps won't damage the bark the way bar clamps can.

CUT ⁵⁄₈-IN.-DIA. TENONS on the cross stretchers for the front and back.

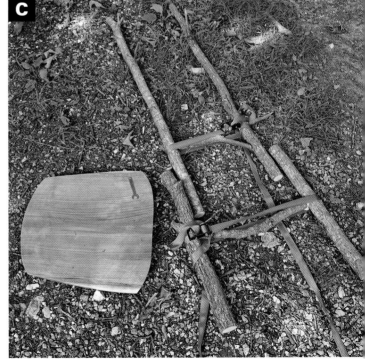

D

USE SCRAP BOARDS AND CLAMPS to hold the front and back legs in position as you measure for side stretchers.

E

DRILL THE ANGLED ⅝-IN. MORTISES in the front and back leg assemblies for the side stretchers. Use the angle you observed when the chair was mocked up. A piece of tape on the drill bit helps guide it to the right depth.

5. Cut tenons on each end of the stretchers (PHOTO **B**).

6. Use band clamps or bar clamps to pull the joints tight after you spread polyurethane glue in the mortises. Then lay the parts flat on the ground or floor as they dry. You will find that by turning the stretchers slightly in their mortises you will find the way they fit best and hold the legs in alignment (PHOTO **C**).

7. Determine the lengths and angles for the side stretchers. Clamp wide boards onto the ends of the front and back leg assemblies. This will allow you to mock up the parts of the chair and figure out the

angles for the mortises in the front and back legs. You can also determine the lengths for the side stretchers. The lengths should make a frame that is slightly too small to fit the top. It also helps you see how you want to angle the seat back (PHOTO **D**).

8. Offset the location of the side-stretcher mortises from the front and back stretchers. You don't want the joints to intersect in the legs. You can either measure their locations directly or use a story stick (PHOTO **E**). The drill angle is not precise but should be an approximation of the angle you saw when the chair was mocked up. Fortunately there is some flex in rustic stock that allows for minor discrepancies in mortise angle.

9. Cut the side stretchers to length and cut tenons on each end.

10. Spread polyurethane glue in the mortises and clamp the chair frame tightly together. It is a good idea at this point to hold the seat up in position and observe how it will fit the frame. If you have done it right, the seat will not fit in the frame yet, either in width or length **(PHOTO F)**.

USE A BAND CLAMP TO HOLD the chair frame together as the glue for the stretchers sets.

Fit and attach the seat

THE WALNUT SEAT IN THIS CHAIR is simply held in place with four 3-in. wood screws. They're driven through the legs into the seat and hidden with walnut plugs. For this system to work, the seat has to be shaped at the corners to conform to the shape of the legs.

1. Hold the seat centered in the chair frame to observe how much you will need to remove from each side to make a good fit **(PHOTO A)**. Then mark what material you need to cut away for the seat to fit the frame. I work on one corner at a time.

2. On the front corners, nibble away a bit with a jigsaw first, being careful not to cut too close to the line. Then use a rasp to smooth the cut right up to the line **(PHOTO B)**. Do the same for each corner in sequence as you fit the seat within the four legs of the chair. Hold the rasp so that it cuts straight up and down. File from the top toward the bottom of the seat to prevent tearout along the top edge.

3. Use a band clamp to hold the chair frame tightly in place as you attach the seat. Measure the height and adjust it so that it's the same at all four corners.

MARK THE WASTE AT EACH CORNER of the seat for fitting it within the frame. I mark and fit one corner at a time.

USE A RASP TO FINE-TUNE the cutouts as required to fit the chair frame.

WITH THE SEAT HELD IN PLACE with a band clamp, drive long screws through the legs into the seat to attach it. Drill and countersink the holes first to avoid splitting and so that the screws can be hidden by dowels.

USE A FINE-TOOTHED SAW TO TRIM the tops of the front legs flush with the seat after it's secure.

4. Use a drill and countersink to drill pilot holes for the screws. Then drive the screws in place. I work on one corner at a time, making certain the leg is nested tightly in the recess before the hole is drilled **(PHOTO C)**.

5. With a fine-toothed handsaw, trim the front legs even with the top surface of the seat **(PHOTO D)**.

Be careful to avoid sawing into the seat. After you make this cut, remove the screws and seat temporarily so the tops of the front legs can be sanded.

6. Trim off the bottom ends of the legs so that the chair will rest evenly on a flat surface. I cut ¾ in. more off the back legs so that the seat and back slope backward.

Make a seat back

IF YOU HAVE ACCESS TO A BANDSAW, use it to shape the seat back. If not, you will have to do more work with the handheld grinder, but it will be manageable.

1. Begin with a piece of wood wide enough for all three parts. You'll shape them at the same time so each will have a matching contour.

2. Saw out the basic curve on a bandsaw. Otherwise, clamp the seat back stock firmly to a flat surface and grind it to shape. As with the seat, your sense of touch is your best guide, and absolute perfection is not required **(PHOTO A)**.

GRIND THE BACK BLANK to a smooth curved shape with a coarse 60-grit disk. I cut this to shape with a bandsaw first, but it can all be done with the grinder if necessary.

3. After you have shaped the seat back, use a random-orbit sander to remove the coarse sander marks and bring it to a final finish **(PHOTO B)**.

4. Cut the seat back into the three parts. This operation can be done safely with a tablesaw, jigsaw, or handsaw. I would avoid using a hand-held circular saw, because it's impossible to hold the stock safely during the cuts.

FINISH SAND THE SEAT BACK with a random-orbit sander after you've shaped it.

WORK SMART

A common spray bottle works well for applying an oil finish to a rough surface such as bark-covered sticks. Spray the surfaces lightly and allow to dry. Excessive oil can drip and run, so should be avoided. Smooth surfaces should be wiped with a soft cloth before the finish dries, about 45 minutes after application.

Shape and attach the seat back

BEFORE FINAL SHAPING AND ATTACHMENT of the seat back, clamp the parts in place so you can step back and make your final design decisions.

1. After mocking up the back on this chair, I reshaped the top and cut the lower pieces a bit shorter. But these are aesthetic decisions and there are no absolutes. Each chair (or other project) you make will offer chances for testing and developing your aesthetic judgment **(PHOTO A)**.

MOCK UP THE CHAIR AND GET a good look at it before screwing the last parts in place. Decide what looks good and what doesn't, then make adjustments.

B

USE A CHISEL TO SHAPE THE BACK legs as needed so the back pieces sit flat.

C

DRILL AND COUNTERSINK HOLES through the back parts into the legs. Countersink deep enough to allow for walnut plugs to hide the screws.

2. If needed, reshape one or both of the back legs with a wide chisel to let the back parts sit flat **(PHOTO B)**.

3. Drill pilot holes through the seat back splats into the back legs and then use screws to attach them in place. I used a countersink bit to drill the holes. After they were screwed tight, I plugged the holes with shop-made walnut plugs. You may choose to do the same, or you can cut short pieces of ⅜-in. dowel for plugs. You can either sand them flush or leave them slightly raised for a more rustic look **(PHOTO C)**.

Variation: Armchair

MAKING AN ARMCHAIR IS ONLY SLIGHTLY different from making a chair without arms. It needs greater width across the front to get in and out easily, it needs longer front legs that rise above the seat, and of course it needs arms. You can make arms from tree branches like the rest of the chair, or use roughsawn lumber like these.

Armchair variation with seagrass
woven seat and cherry arms

There are thousands of ways to modify a basic rustic chair. You can change the seating material, or add arms and a woven back. This one with a woven seagrass seat and back and cherry arms is just one example. The very best may come from your imagination.

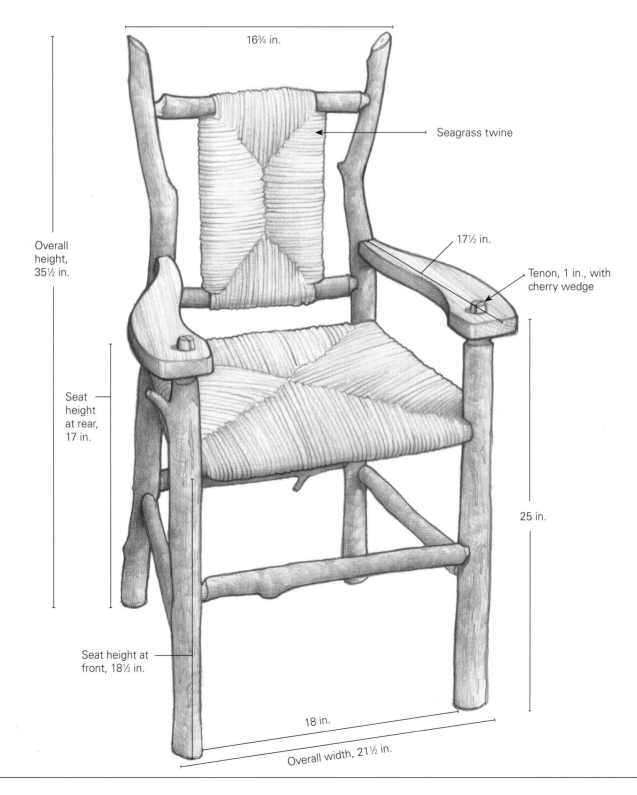

16¾ in.

Seagrass twine

17½ in.

Tenon, 1 in., with cherry wedge

Overall height, 35½ in.

Seat height at rear, 17 in.

25 in.

Seat height at front, 18½ in.

18 in.

Overall width, 21½ in.

MATERIALS FOR ARMCHAIR VARIATION

QUANTITY	PART	ROUGH SIZE	FINISHED SIZE	MATERIAL	NOTES
2	Back legs	1½ in. dia. by 37½ in.	1½ in. dia. by 35½ in.	Hickory	
2	Front legs	1¾ in. dia. by 27 in.	1¾ in. dia. by 25 in.	Hickory	
2	Front stretchers		1¼ in. dia. by 20 in.	Hickory	
3	Back stretchers		1⅛ in. to 1¼ in. dia. by varying lengths	Hickory	
2	Back supports		1 in. dia. by 12½ in.	Hickory	
4	Side stretchers		1¼ in. dia. by 16 in.	Hickory	
2	Arms		1 in. by 4 in. by 17 in.	Cherry	
3	Seagrass twine	1-lb. rolls, 4.5 mm to 5 mm dia.			Available from www.seatweaving.org
4	Furniture glides	⅞ in.			Available from www.allglides.com, stock number SG87

Make the chair and design the arms

1. I begin by building the chair using the same joinery techniques as used in making the chair with the walnut seat.

2. When you've assembled everything except the arms, place a board across the stretchers so you can sit and judge the height the arms should be placed. Of course, this judgment could be made differently according to the taste of the individual maker.

3. Cut tenons on the ends of the front legs to set the height you like.

4. Measure for arms long enough to fit over the tenons and reach the chair back, and add the length of a tenon to fit into the back leg.

Make and attach the arm

USE ONE ARM AS A TEMPLATE for the second. This ensures a good symmetry between the arms.

USE A ROTARY CHISEL TO PROVIDE texture to the edges of the chair arms. Tap the tool lightly as you move it over the surface of the wood for a hand-carved look.

1. Sketch the shape of the arm on a blank. Saw it out using a jigsaw and shape it as you like. When it's finished, use it as a template for the other arm (PHOTO **A**).

2. You can sand and smooth the edges of the arms for contrast with the rest of the chair or gently texture them with a rotary chisel (see the sidebar on p. 87) (PHOTO **B**).

3. Measure, mark, and cut a hole in the arm that's the same diameter as the tenon on the end of the front leg.

4. Fit the arm on the tenon and mark the point at which to drill the mortise in the back leg (PHOTO **C**). Slide the arm out of the way when drilling the mortise.

5. Cut the arm to length and use the Veritas tenoner to form a tenon on the end. Before attaching the arm to the chair, sand it.

6. Use a handsaw to cut a groove across the end of both leg tenons so that you can lock the tenons with wedges later.

MARK THE INTERSECTION BETWEEN the arm and back leg on both parts.

7. Spread glue in the mortises and on the tenons and inside the mortises drilled in the arms. Then jiggle the arms in place and clamp them in position.

8. Cut and insert a wedge of wood into the slots cut in the front legs to lock the tenons in the arms (as shown on pp. 50–51).

9. Finish the chair with two coats of Danish oil.

WORK SMART

Straight stock is easiest to work and makes successful chairs. But wildly crooked stock produces the most interesting work. Learn the basics with the use of straight stock and save the most interesting stock and greatest challenge for later.

Make a seagrass seat

It is easy to make a seagrass or Shaker tape seat for a rustic chair following the directions in "Rustic Tree Branch Footstool" on p. 66. However, unlike a rectangular footstool, this chair is wider at the front than at the back, so the front corners must be filled first. This requires some additional steps.

1. On a seagrass-twine seat, begin by weaving just the left corner, across the front, and then the right corner, over and over until the open width measured across the front and back stretchers is the same **(PHOTO A)**. Do this with several short pieces. Tack one to the left stretcher, bring it over the front stretcher, then up and over the left stretch and then over the right stretcher, then over the front stretcher and then tack the end to the right side stretcher. The key to remember is always to go over the stretcher with the twine, never under.

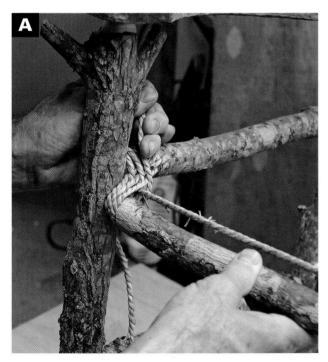

FILL THE FRONT CORNERS WITH SHORT STRIPS of grass. Use tacks to attach each length of twine to the left seat stretcher, wrap it over the front, over itself on the side, over the right stretcher, and over the front, and then use a tack to attach it to the right stretcher.

WHEN YOU'VE FILLED IN THE FRONT corners with short twine pieces, you'll have a square or rectangle of empty space left. Finish the seagrass seat using the technique shown in "Rustic Tree Branch Footstool" on p. 66.

WEAVE THE SEAT BACK USING the same technique as on the seat.

2. When the shape of the open space remaining is rectangular and no longer wider at the front, weave the rest of the seat as described in "Rustic Tree Branch Footstool" on p. 66 **(PHOTO B)**.

3. For the seat back, use the same technique. When weaving a space that is rectangular, weave in the same manner until the short sides are complete. Then finish by weaving in a figure-eight pattern until the space is all filled **(PHOTO C)**.

Rustic White Oak Chest

THIS RUSTIC CHEST and the small cabinet variations are made with a simple process of gluing alternating lengths of roughsawn wood so they overlap where they meet at the corners. Here I use the stock on edge rather than flat, but the joints are very much like those used in building a log cabin.

There are things I like about this joinery technique. The first is that it is easy to do. I also like that it is so obvious how it works. I used screws covered by ⅜-in. walnut dowels to lock the corners together and to create an even more rustic effect. To make the interior smooth and hospitable to blankets and linens, and also to lighten the weight of the finished chest, I planed the material to a uniform thickness before assembly. Keep the most interesting rough and rustic faces on the outside. The roughsawn surface lends itself to an "ebonizing" process to increase the old weathered oak look as done here or offers the opportunity to play with milk paints, as used in "Five-Board Bench" on p. 16.

Rustic white oak chest

In this white oak chest, edge-glued lengths of narrow stock create the log-cabin-style corner joints. The roughsawn wood is treated with an ebonizing solution of steel wool dissolved in vinegar, then sanded for an aged look. An interior tray, manila rope pulls, and a lid support complete the chest, giving it a nautical look.

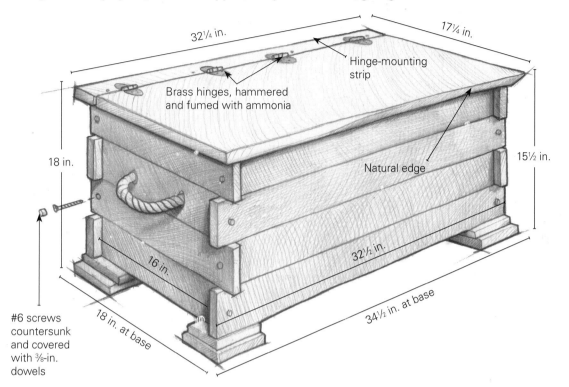

32¼ in.

17¼ in.

Hinge-mounting strip

Brass hinges, hammered and fumed with ammonia

Natural edge

18 in.

15½ in.

16 in.

32½ in.

#6 screws countersunk and covered with ⅜-in. dowels

18 in. at base

34½ in. at base

Interior details

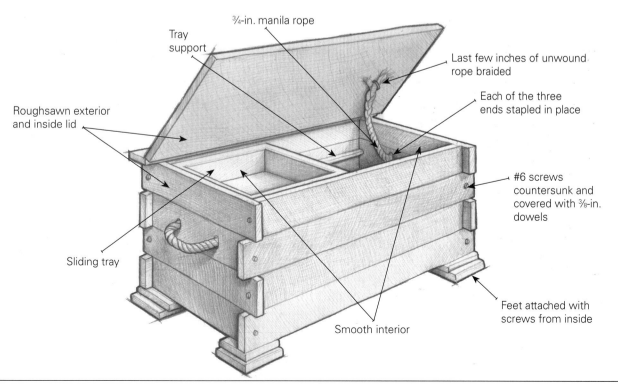

¾-in. manila rope

Tray support

Last few inches of unwound rope braided

Roughsawn exterior and inside lid

Each of the three ends stapled in place

#6 screws countersunk and covered with ⅜-in. dowels

Sliding tray

Smooth interior

Feet attached with screws from inside

MATERIALS FOR RUSTIC WHITE OAK CHEST

QUANTITY	PART	SIZE	MATERIAL	NOTES
4	Parts for front and back	¾ in. by 3⅞ in. by 32½ in.	White oak	*
4	Parts for front and back	¾ in. by 3⅞ in. by 30 in.	White oak	*
4	Parts for end	¾ in. by 3⅞ in. by 16 in.	White oak	*
4	Parts for end	¾ in. by 3⅞ in. by 13½ in.	White oak	*
1	Bottom	½ in. by 14¼ in. by 30¾ in.	Baltic birch plywood	1/32 in. smaller in each dimension to ease fit
1	Hinge-mounting strip	1 in. by 2 in. by 33¼ in.		**
1	Lid	1 in. by 17¼ in. by 33¼ in.		**
24	Walnut plugs	⅜ in. by ⅜ in.	Walnut	Available from www.rockler.com
2	Top foot panels	⅝ in. by 1¾ in. by 6 in.	White oak	*
2	Top foot panels	⅝ in. by 1¾ in. by 11 in.	White oak	*
4	Bottom foot panels	⅝ in. by 1¾ in. by 3½ in.	White oak	*
4	Bottom foot panels	⅝ in. by 1¾ in. by 4½ in.	White oak	*
2	Tray fronts and backs	¾ in. by 5 in. by 16 in.	White oak	Planed all sides
2	Tray ends	¾ in. by 5 in. by 13¼ in.	White oak	Planed all sides
1	Tray bottom	¼ in. by 12½ in. by 15¼ in.	Baltic birch plywood	Available from home centers
2 pair	Hinges	1 5/16 in. by 2⅞ in.	Brass	
24	Screws	¾-in. #4 flathead	Brass	
20	Screws	1⅝-in. #6 drywall, countersunk	Steel	
4 ft.	Rope	¾ in.	Manila	Available from hardware stores

* Planed on one side only

** Left unplaned and roughsawn, both sides

Prepare the stock

B

GANG-PLANE THE JOINTED BOARDS to a common width. Hold the boards together as they are pulled into the planer, and then grasp them tightly together as they emerge on the other side.

MANY WOODWORKERS PREFER TO BUY their materials already planed so they can see the beauty of the figure and grain. But the markings left by the sawmill are interesting and tell a story of their own. When you buy roughsawn lumber, you can choose how much of that interesting story will be left to tell by your finished work.

1. Begin by planing your stock to uniform thickness. The white oak I used was a full inch thick, so I planed it down to ¾ in. Always keep the roughest and most interesting side down away from the blades.

2. Rip the wood to width. You will find this is easiest using a tablesaw, but it can also be done with a circular saw and ripping guide, as shown in "Western Cedar Tables" on p. 4.

C

CROSSCUT THE BOARDS TO THEIR FINISHED lengths. I use a sled on the tablesaw for the most accurate results.

3. The boards must be straight enough to get a good glue joint between them. After ripping, I straighten each board by jointing one edge **(PHOTO A)**. Then I pass them through the planer all together on edge to make them uniform in width **(PHOTO B)**. These steps can be done with a hand-plane and circular saw with ripping guide, but this involves both more skill and more work.

4. Cut the boards to length. I use a crosscut sled on the tablesaw and a stop block clamped in place to ensure accurate cuts **(PHOTO C)** .

A

EDGE-JOIN EACH BOARD. A power jointer is most effective, particularly where the boards may be slightly warped.

BUYING ROUGHSAWN LUMBER

Most retail lumber companies these days sell their wood surfaced on both sides, making it easier to see its color and quality. The extra service also enables the retailer to sell the wood for more money. But for rustic work you will have other design objectives that may lead you to go shopping outside your usual sources. With the invention sev-eral years ago of trailer-mounted bandsaw mills, most communities large and small have someone harvesting lumber from local trees. Call your community arborist or tree-trimmer for possible sources of roughsawn lumber. Remember, however, to dry your wood before use. In dry storage, it takes one year per inch of thickness.

Assemble and sand the sides

GLUING THE PARTS TOGETHER TO FORM the ends and sides requires special care. You will find that your sense of touch will be useful in this operation.

1. Set the four boards for one side together. Use a square to check that the short parts are in perfect alignment. A carpenter's square works best because of its size.

2. Spread glue on the edges of the short boards, press the parts together, then check and double-check as you apply clamping pressure (**PHOTO A**). Spread glue on the edges of the short boards but not the long ones, to keep glue off the log-cabin joints. Parts can slide around as you apply clamping pressure, so check again with the square that the edges align before you set the assembly aside for the glue to dry.

3. Use a scraper to remove excess dried glue. Then sand from coarse to fine. I start with 120 grit in a random-orbit sander and finish with 320 grit (**PHOTO B**).

A

WHILE GLUING THE SIDES, check and recheck the edges using a square to make certain the short boards align perfectly with each other. As you apply clamping pressure, the boards can shift slightly, so do a final check on alignment before you step away to wait for the glue to dry.

B

SAND THE INSIDES OF THE CHEST after the glue has dried, moving from coarse to fine grits.

WORK SMART

Glued boards can slide against each other as you apply clamping pressure, so check and check again that the boards are in the exact position required. Then check again before setting the wood and clamps aside to dry. It can be frustrating getting things just right, but it's worse to come back an hour or more later and discover things are not assembled the way you want.

Fit the bottom panel

I USE A PLUNGE ROUTER TO CUT both the grooves for the bottom panel and the grooves for the tray support strips. A plunge router is the best tool for these operations because it can start and stop without exiting through the end of the stock.

1. Mark the start and end of the cut about ¾ in. in from each end of the front and back. Set the fence so the bit cuts ½ in. from the edge.

2. At the left end of the workpiece, put the plunge router in position with the fence against the edge. Then, with the router turned on, plunge the bit into the end of the cut. Moving from left to right is essential, as the rotation of the router bit will pull the router and fence tight to the workpiece. I prefer to make the cut in steps, gradually lowering the router to full depth in increments. Making a full-depth cut in one pass makes the small router bit work too hard and risks breaking it **(PHOTO A)**.

A

USE A PLUNGE ROUTER WITH A ¼-in.-dia. straight bit to cut a groove for the bottom. Don't cut past the ends to keep the groove hidden after final assembly.

B

USE A PLUNGE ROUTER to cut the groove for the tray support. Make several partial-depth passes, ensuring the fence holds tight against the workpiece. In this photo you can also see the groove for the bottom.

3. Reset the position of the router fence and cut the grooves for the tray supports to fit **(PHOTO B)**. I set the space between the router fence and the bit at a distance of 5 in. to allow for the height of the tray planned for the inside.

4. Use a ⅜-in. rabbeting bit in a fixed-base router to cut the edges of the Baltic birch plywood bottom. Adjust the depth of the cut until the remaining tongue fits in the groove **(PHOTO C)**.

USE A ³/₈-IN. RABBETING BIT TO CUT the bottom panel edge. Adjust the depth of cut until the tongue will fit the groove in the sides of the chest.

Assemble the chest

USE CLAMPS TO HOLD THE FRONT and back tight to the ends as you drive screws in place. I countersink the screws deep enough that I can use walnut dowels to fill the holes and hide the screws.

ADD THE HINGE-MOUNTING STRIP at the back of the chest, using glue and countersunk wood screws to hold it in place. A bit of wax on the screws will ease their passage into the wood.

AT THIS POINT THE FOUR SIDES of the chest should fit easily together, the joints coming together like your fingers when you clasp your hands.

1. Check the corners for any glue squeeze-out that might keep the pieces from pulling tight. Use a chisel to remove any excess glue.

2. Use bar clamps to hold the sides together while you drive screws across the joints to pull the parts tight **(PHOTO A)**. The screw holes should be countersunk. You can fill the holes later with walnut dowels for an even more rustic look.

3. After you set the first set of screws from one direction, remove the clamps, turn the chest 90 degrees, and install screws from the other direction. Don't add the walnut dowels yet. Wait until after you treat the sides with the ebonizing solution and sand them smooth.

4. Attach the hinge-mounting strip at the back edge of the chest. Predrill and countersink holes for the screws and drill deep enough that walnut dowels can be used to hide the screws **(PHOTO B)**.

Make the rustic feet

A **USE GLUE AND A NAIL GUN** to connect the parts for the feet. Note how the corners overlap, log-cabin style.

B **USE A GRINDER OR RASP TO SHAPE** and roughen the edges of the foot assembly. Clamp it tight to a table or workbench. Avoid the temptation to hold it in your hand.

I MAKE THE FOUR FEET AS A SINGLE unit first, then cut them apart later. This makes assembly and texturing easier.

1. Cut the parts to length and align them to overlap at the corners. Apply glue, then hold each piece in position as you nail it in place (**PHOTO A**).

2. Once the foot assembly is complete, use a rasp or grinder to shape the edges. Rough, random markings should contrast with smoother strokes of the grinder or rasp. I use the edge of the sander to make marks on the end-grain wood (**PHOTO B**).

3. Once the texturing is complete, use a handsaw to cut the assembly into four individual feet. A Japanese dozuki saw makes an easy, accurate cut (**PHOTO C**).

4. Attach the feet to the assembled chest by driving countersunk screws through the plywood bottom of the chest into the carefully positioned feet.

C **USE A HANDSAW TO CUT** the foot assembly into four separate feet.

Make a tray

USE THE TABLESAW TO CUT GROOVES in the tray sides for the bottom to fit. Move the fence over to widen the cut until the ¼-in. Baltic birch plywood bottom fits.

WORK SMART

When using a plywood bottom, put a bit of glue in the grooves at the corners to add strength to the box.

TILT THE BLADE ON THE TABLESAW to 45 degrees and cut the parts for the tray to length. Use a stop block on the miter gauge to make sure that the tray ends and front and back are equal in size.

I MAKE A SLIDING TRAY FROM PLANED WHITE OAK TO FIT inside the chest. The smooth surface of the tray and of the interior of the chest make a great contrast with the rustic exterior.

1. Use a tablesaw to miter the corners of the dimensioned stock for the sides of the box. I use a stop block on the miter gauge to make certain that the front and back and the paired ends are of equal lengths **(PHOTO A)**.

2. On the tablesaw cut grooves for the bottom panel. You can either use a dado blade to cut a ¼-in.-wide groove or use a narrower blade and gradually widen the cut by changing the setting of the fence **(PHOTO B)**.

3. Cut the bottom panel to size and then sand the inside of all the parts before assembly.

4. Clamping mitered corners is difficult to do with standard clamps but very easy with common clear plastic packing tape. I arrange the boards the way they will go together in the finished piece, then turn them over and apply glue on the mitered surfaces. Then I stretch clear package-sealing tape over the corners to pull them tight. Apply additional layers of tape as needed, pulling each layer tight **(PHOTO C)**. Examine the corners closely to see that any gaps have completely closed. If no amount of strength will pull the joint tight, check the size of the bottom. It may be too large.

5. After the glue has dried, sand the outside of the tray and use a nail gun to shoot finish nails into the corners to provide extra strength.

6. Install the tray supports inside the box with glue and screws. Align them so the top of the tray rests just below the top edge of the chest.

C

USE TAPE TO PULL THE CORNERS tight as you assemble the tray. Don't skimp on tape. Each layer will add clamping pressure. Make sure all the corners are pulled tight before you set the tray aside for the glue to dry.

Texture, stain, and sand the chest

A

USE THE GRINDER AND COARSE SANDING DISK to make the corners and edges more rustic in texture. Dig the edge in randomly to get the best results. You can also do this job effectively with a rasp or sanding block.

MUCH OF THE VISUAL INTEREST of this chest comes from the roughsawn texture left by the saw-mill. So far I've only sanded the interior, where I want a smooth surface to make the chest more inviting for use. On the exterior, I delay sanding until after applying an ebonizing solution of steel wool and vinegar (see "Western Cedar Tables" on p. 4). This accentuates the texture. Sanding will make the exterior of the chest feel soft and inviting to the touch.

1. Wear away all the exposed edges using a grinder with a coarse sanding disk or with a smooth rasp. Dig in with the edges of the tool for extra texture, and attempt to be somewhat random rather than regular in your motions **(PHOTO A)**.

2. Apply masking tape to the top edges of the box to prevent the ebonizing solution from staining them. As you spray, carefully avoid staining any part

B

USE A SPRAY BOTTLE WITH EBONIZING SOLUTION to stain the chest. Mask the edges with tape to avoid staining the interior.

C

AFTER THE SOLUTION HAS DARKENED THE WOOD and become completely dry, use a random-orbit sander to sand through the ebonizing in the high spots. Also sand lightly in the low spots to make the chest smooth to the touch.

D

SCREW THE HINGES IN PLACE on the mounting strip. Then put the lid in place and attach the hinges to it. Note the block of wood with holes drilled in it to hold the screws while they were being fumed with ammonia.

that you want to keep in a natural oak color. I use a common spray bottle to apply the solution (**PHOTO B**). Test the ebonizing solution on scrapwood before spraying the chest. If the scrapwood turns too dark, dilute the solution with water until you get the effect you want.

E

USE A RANDOM-ORBIT SANDER to sand the surface and reveal the natural wood tones underneath the ebonizing. By tilting the sander slightly into low spots, they can be made smooth to the touch without sanding through the color too much.

Certainly, most people want brass hinges to look shiny and new. But when you are making rustic furniture, a bright brass hinge stands out like a hammered and bandaged thumb. However, you can easily "antique" the look of brass with a common household cleaning solution: ammonia.

First, use lacquer thinner and steel wool to remove any protective coating on the hinges. Then pour a few ounces of ammonia from the cleaning-supplies section of your local grocery store in a large resealable storage bag. Place the hinges on a block of wood inside the bag, close the bag, then let the ammonia do its work. If you need to treat screws, drill oversize holes in a piece of wood and insert the screws so they stand up about half or a third of the way out of the wood. Don't worry if some liquid gets on the metal. It won't hurt the process. But it's the fumes that will do the work. Also, be aware that ammonia fumes are toxic. Do your treatment outdoors and wear gloves.

When the hinges and screws have developed enough patina, remove them from the bag. I also hammered the hinges lightly with a waffle-faced framing hammer to give them more of a handmade appearance before the patina was applied.

This technique will only work on real brass, not brass-plated or brass-colored hinges. Even real brass hinges may come with brass-plated screws.

TREAT THE BRASS HINGES WITH AMMONIA to make them look old. I put the hinges on a block of wood, put a paper towel in a plastic resealable bag, and pour common household ammonia inside. Don't breathe the fumes or allow the ammonia to get on your hands. This technique will only work on solid brass.

Ammonia will completely dissolve brass plating, so use solid brass screws.

Apply Danish oil to your finished work and the hinges after they are in place. The oil finish will help protect the patina.

3. Spray all edges and sides of the top with ebonizing solution. After the color turns and the wood dries, use a random-orbit sander with 220 grit to smooth the wood. By sanding the high spots, you reveal some of the natural color beneath the ebonized surface. Also sand the low spots lightly to make the whole surface more smooth and inviting to touch **(PHOTO C)**.

4. Drill pilot holes for the hinges in the lid and mounting strip. I use a Vix bit, which self-centers in the holes and drills to the correct depth. Then set the screws. A thin coating of wax will help the screws to go in without stripping the heads **(PHOTO D)**.

5. Use an orbital sander to sand the rest of the cabinet **(PHOTO E)**.

Finish the chest

I USE DEFT DANISH OIL AS A PROTECTIVE
coating and to bring out the depth of color in the
wood. The rope pulls and lid stop add an even more
rustic touch. I used coarse hemp rope, which can be
purchased by the foot at a local hardware store, to
give the chest a nautical look.

1. Use a spray bottle to coat the chest inside and
out with Danish oil **(PHOTO A)**. Apply the oil liberally, then wait 20 minutes and apply a second coat.
After that coat has dried for 30 to 40 minutes use
a dry cloth to wipe down the chest, inside and out.
Also apply Danish oil to the interior tray. Using a
spray bottle to apply the finish is easier than using
a brush or cloth because of the textured surface on
the outside of the chest

2. Drill ⅞-in. holes in the ends of the chest for the
rope handles to fit. I use an auger bit with a spur
on the outside of the cut so that the edges will be
smooth. Drill just partway through from the outside. When you see the center point of the drill
beginning to emerge from the other side, finish the
hole by drilling from the inside. Drilling in from
both sides will reduce the probability of tearout
(PHOTO B).

3. Attach the rope on the inside of the chest. First
untwist the end of the rope and then braid it for
a few inches so that the rope terminates in three
parts. Use electrical staples to attach each end of
the braid to the underside of the lid. Then weave
it through the holes in the chest before stapling the
other end to the inside of the chest **(PHOTO C)**.
You will need to drill pilot holes for the points of
the staples if working with white oak or a wood
as hard.

SPRAY DANISH OIL FINISH ON THE CHEST,
inside and out, with a spray bottle. Apply two coats 20 to
35 minutes apart, then rub the surface with a dry cloth. A
second application and wiping 24 hours later will create a
perfect finish.

DRILL THROUGH THE SIDES FOR THE ROPE handles to fit. Drill only partway from the outside. When the
tip of the drill bit starts to enter the inside, finish the hole
by drilling from the inside. This will prevent tearout.

ATTACH EACH END OF THE MANILA ROPE stay
to the lid, using large staples. Predrilling is necessary in
woods as hard as this oak.

Variation: Rustic wall cabinet

TO MAKE THE RUSTIC WALL cabinet, follow the same steps used in building the rustic chest. To reduce the weight, I plane the wood thinner, down to ⅝ in. thick, and I use ¼-in. Baltic birch plywood in place of the heavier ½-in. material. I add a ⅜-in.-thick hanger strip on the back so that it can be easily hung on the wall. And I drill holes inside for adjustable shelf supports to fit. Rather than a single door as used in the rustic chest, I cut the doors from a single plank of contrasting hickory, plane and sand them smooth, and orient them with the natural bark edge where the doors meet.

Rustic wall cabinet variation

This red oak cabinet has the same basic construction as the chest but is set on end. The doors are hickory with natural bark edges.

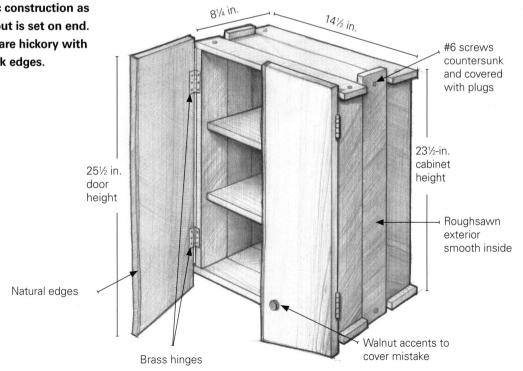

8¼ in.

14½ in.

#6 screws countersunk and covered with plugs

23½-in. cabinet height

25½ in. door height

Roughsawn exterior smooth inside

Natural edges

Brass hinges

Walnut accents to cover mistake

MATERIALS FOR RUSTIC WALL CABINET VARIATION

QUANTITY	PART	SIZE	MATERIAL	NOTES
2	Long parts for sides	⅝ in. by 2½ in. by 23½ in.	Red oak	*
4	Short parts or sides	⅝ in. by 2½ in. by 21 in.	Red oak	*
4	Long parts for top and bottom	⅝ in. by 2½ in. by 15¾ in.	Red oak	*
2	Short parts for top and bottom	⅝ in. by 2½ in. by 13¼ in.	Red oak	*
1	Back	¼ in. by 13¾ in. by 21½ in.	Baltic birch plywood	
2	Doors	¾ in. by 7⅛ in. by 25⅝ in.	Hickory	Cut from single board with bark edges
2	Shelves	7⁄16 in. by 6¾ in. by 13³⁄16 in.	Red oak	Planed both sides
2 pair	Hinges	2 in. by 1⅜ in.	Brass	Ives, #C9042B5, available at home centers
4	Magnets	3 mm by 10 mm dia.	Rare earth	Available from Woodcraft Supply, #128471
2	Hanger strips	½ in. by 3 in. by 13³⁄16 in.	Hardwood	Cut each with 35-degree angle on one long edge.
12	Screws	1¼-in. #6 drywall		
12	Plugs	⅜ in. dia. by ⅜ in.	Walnut	Available from www.rockler.com
8	Shelf supports	¼ in.	Antique brass-plated steel	Available from Woodcraft Supply, #27116, or Rockler, #33902

* Roughsawn, planed on one side only

1. To make a small cabinet, follow the same steps used in making a chest. However, drill holes for the shelf supports before you assemble it. Also note the recess at the back of the cabinet that allows room for the hanger strip for mounting the cabinet to the wall.

2. Mark and drill the shelf support holes. Use an accurate square and measure carefully **(PHOTO A)**. The drilling can be done with either a drill press or hand-held electric drill. The drill press will give the most accurate results. With the hand-held drill, put a piece of tape as a gauge on the drill bit to prevent

MARK THE LOCATIONS FOR SHELF HOLES carefully so the shelves will rest level in the cabinet.

B

USE A JIGSAW OR HANDSAW to cut the door panels from a single board.

C

drilling too deep. Mark the holes for drilling with an awl to prevent the drill from wandering, and be careful that the drill is held perpendicular to the stock.

3. For the doors, rip a single board to divide it into two matched door panels. This can be done with a jigsaw, circular saw, or handsaw (**PHOTO B**). Then plane the doors down on both sides to provide contrast with the cabinet sides. If you prefer a more rustic look, just plane the stock on the inside.

4. Center the doors on the assembled cabinet. Mark the outside edges to cut them down to size (**PHOTO C**).

USE A PENCIL TO MARK THE LINE OF CUT on each side after you lay the door boards in place centered on the cabinet. Then trim away the waste and join the edges smooth.

5. To install the hinges, first make a routing template as shown. Use pieces of ¼-in.-thick plywood in pieces that equal the length and closed width of the hinge. This jig can be reused whenever you use hinges of the same size. You use it to guide the router while cutting the butt hinge mortises in both the doors and the cabinet sides (**PHOTO D**).

You can avoid this complicated process by using external-mount hinges as on the rustic chest. But if you want to lessen the visibility of your hardware, this is an easy way to do it. Use a bearing-guided mortise clean-out bit in a laminate trimmer. The bearing at the top follows the shape of the template, routing the space for the hinge to fit (**PHOTO E**).

6. Drill pilot holes for the screws. If using brass screws, apply wax to the threads to lubricate them for easy installation. Install the screws (**PHOTO F**).

7. I hide magnets in the doors to serve as catches. Drill holes of the same diameter as the disk magnets in the back sides of the doors (**PHOTO G**). Carefully mark the place on the cabinet where the magnet will hit and drill for another magnet to fit in the front edge of the cabinet bottom.

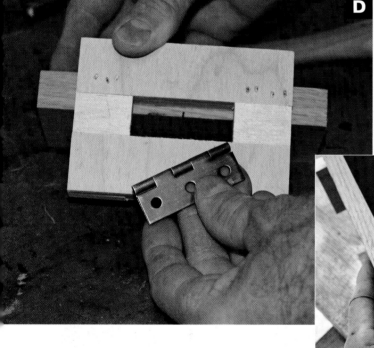

D

MAKE A SIMPLE ROUTING JIG for installing the butt hinges like the one shown. The interior space is the exact size of the hinge. The block on the underside positions the jig in the right place, controlling how much of the hinge barrel protrudes on the outside of the cabinet.

CLAMP THE JIG IN PLACE and then use a bearing-guided mortise cleanout bit to remove the waste. The bearing at the top of the bit follows the jig, duplicating its shape in the wood, and the depth of the bit controls the depth of the mortise.

E

USE WAX ON THE THREADS as you install the hinges for the doors.

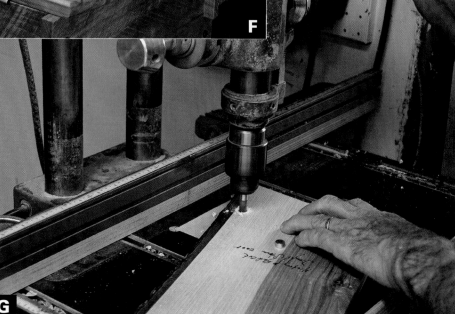

USE A DRILL PRESS TO CUT HOLES to install magnets to serve as cabinet catches on each door and in the front edges of the cabinet. Careful measurement is required to make sure they align with each other. Make sure when you glue the magnets in place that they are in position to attract rather than repel.

OOPS! DESIGN FEATURE!

Many woodworkers like me have learned to regard errors as opportunities. I have learned some of my best techniques while recovering from mistakes. For example, in making this chest I drilled a hole for a magnet on the wrong side of the door. I could find a new board and start over. Or I could try to fill and repair the hole with a piece of matching wood. Or I could turn the mistake into a "design feature" by adding a piece of contrasting wood as a design element to both doors.

You can see what I decided. Does it work? You get to be the judge. I can tell you that my decision had two components. First, I had no more of the same wood. Second, anything I did to try to fix it would still be somewhat visible and in a conspicuous spot. Anyway, I like how it turned out. Let's keep this to ourselves, however.

Hang the cabinet

Hanging a small cabinet can be a big challenge or easy as pie. I prefer pie.

1. Plane a board to the thickness of the space between the cabinet back and the back edge of the wood. For this cabinet, the material needs to be ½ in. thick. The board should be cut to a length equal to the width between the two sides at the back of the cabinet.

SET THE TABLE-SAW BLADE ANGLE between 35 and 45 degrees and rip the hanger stock into two pieces.

MOUNT THE HANGER STRIP AT THE TOP of the back of the cabinet with construction adhesive.

2. Rip the hanger stock into two pieces with the blade tilted between 35 and 45 degrees **(PHOTO A)**.

3. Cut the hanger strips to length so that they fit between the cabinet sides. Glue one piece of the hanger strip to the back of the cabinet **(PHOTO B)**. Before the glue sets, turn the cabinet over and set screws through the plywood back for extra strength.

4. Orient the bevel edge with the acute angle out and facing down.

5. Position the other half of the hanger strip on the wall at the desired height and use screws to attach it. The bevel edge should face up and the acute angle face out. Countersink the screws so that they sit flush. After the first screw, check the strip with a level and adjust before you set the second screw. At least one screw should go in a stud.

6. To mount the cabinet, the two angled edges will interlock, securing your cabinet firmly to the wall.

Variation: Freestanding rustic cabinet

CABINETMAKER JAMES KRENOV IS WELL KNOWN for his small freestanding cabinets. Although his work is highly refined, even something as rustic as this can express the deep engagement in the qualities of the materials for which his work is known. Add simple contrasting wood legs to a small cabinet, and you pay homage to the Krenov design legacy without investing the years required to attain the skills expressed in Krenov's work.

Neo–rustic freestanding cabinet variation

With contrasting colors and textures, small freestanding cabinets of this type were made popular by American craftsman James Krenov. More simply and roughly made than those of master cabinetmaker Krenov, this cabinet continues his discussion of wood, and its qualities, colors, and textures.

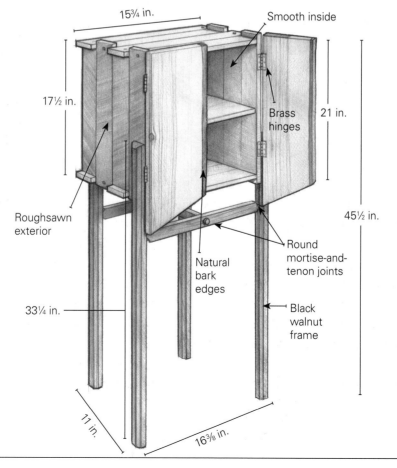

15¾ in.

Smooth inside

17½ in.

Brass hinges

21 in.

Roughsawn exterior

Natural bark edges

Round mortise-and-tenon joints

45½ in.

Black walnut frame

33¼ in.

11 in.

16⅜ in.

MATERIALS FOR FREE STANDING RUSTIC CABINET

QUANTITY	PART	SIZE	MATERIAL	NOTES
4	Long parts for sides	⅝ in. by 2½ in. by 17½ in.	Red oak	*
4	Short parts for sides	⅝ in by 2½ in. by 15 in.	Red oak	*
4	Long parts for top and bottom	⅝ in. by 2½ in. by 15¾ in.	Red oak	*
4	Short parts for top and bottom	⅝ in. by 2½ in. by 13¼ in.	Red oak	*
1	Back	½ in. by 13¾ in. by 15½ in.	Baltic birch plywood	¼-in. by ¼-in. rabbet at each edge
2	Doors	¾ in. by 7⅛ in. by 21 in.	Hickory	Cut from single board with bark edges
1	Shelf	⁷⁄₁₆ in. by 9¼ in. by 13³⁄₁₆ in.	Red oak	Planed both sides
4	Legs	1½ in. by 1½ in. by 33 in.	Walnut	Cut octagonal
1	Front stretcher	¾ in. by 1⅜ in. by 15¼ in.	Walnut	
1	Back stretcher	¾ in. by 1⅜ in. by 12¼ in.	Walnut	
1	Front-to-back stretcher	¾ in. by 1⅜ in. by 10⅞ in.	Walnut	
2 pair	Hinges	2 in. by 1⅜ in.	Brass	Ives, #C9042B5, available at home centers
4	Magnets	3 mm by 10 mm dia.	Rare earth	Available from Woodcraft Supply, #128471
12	Screws	1¼-in. #6 drywall		
12	Plugs	⅜ in. dia. by ⅜ in.	Walnut	
8	Shelf supports	¼ in.	Antique brass	Available from Woodcraft Supply, #27I16, or Rockler, #33902
4	Furniture glides	⅞ in.		Available from www.allglides.com, stock number SG87

* Roughsawn, planed on one side only

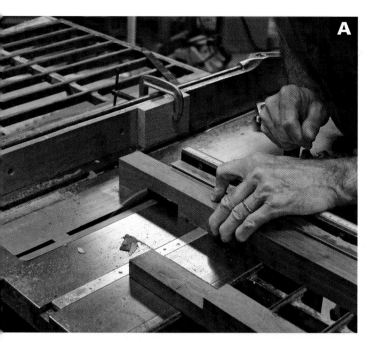

B

DRILL THE MORTISES FOR THE CROSS STRETCH-ERS in the legs. These need to be carefully measured. Check and double-check the locations before drilling.

CUT THE SHOULDERS ON THE LEGS on a table-saw to fit the sides and back of the cabinet. I use a blade that leaves a square-top cut. A dado blade would also work. A stop block clamped to the rip fence ensures the shoulder cuts are all the same length.

FORM TENONS ON THE ENDS of the cross stretchers using a lathe.

1. Mill the leg stock square and then square the ends to make sure the next steps can be done accurately.

2. The legs fit against the sides of the box. To fit them, set the tablesaw blade ⅝ in. high and nibble away the shoulder of the stock (**PHOTO A**). Start with the stock against a stop block clamped to the fence to control the position of the cut, then take successive cuts out to the leg's end. Do this for each of the four legs.

3. To cut the legs to an octagonal shape, use the technique shown on p. 48. Tilt the blade of the table-saw to 45 degrees and cut the corners of the stock.

4. Drill holes in the legs for the tenons on the cross stretchers. Mark and drill the legs carefully so that the mortises will be in perfect alignment (**PHOTO B**).

5. Use a lathe to form tenons on the ends of the cross stretchers (**PHOTO C**). I use a ⅝-in. open-end wrench as my gauge for checking the diameter of the tenons. When the wrench will fit over the tenon, the tenon should fit in the ⅝-in. mortise as well **(PHOTO D)**. A Veritas tenoner will also work for this, but takes special care to align.

6. Spread glue in the mortises and then assemble the frame. It is best to assemble it around the cabinet to make certain that it fits **(PHOTO E)**. Check by measuring to make certain that the legs are spread apart at the bottom the same amount as at the top.

7. Complete the cabinet by adding shelves and doors.

ASSEMBLE THE BASE FRAME with glue in the mortises, draw the clamps tight, and then double-check the fit of the frame on the cabinet. This will square the frame and make certain there will be no difficulties in attaching it to the case after the glue dries.

USE A ⅝-IN. OPEN-END WRENCH as a gauge for exact size. If the wrench fits on the tenon, the tenon will fit the ⅝-in. mortise.